S0-CAU-124

3

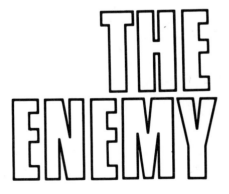

THE
ENEMY

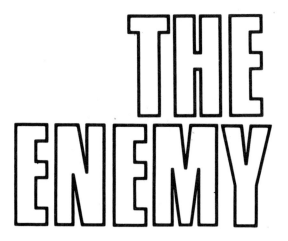

THE ENEMY

SATAN'S STRUGGLE FOR TWO BOYS' SOULS

16985

by TIM and BETSY X

as told to

JIM GRANT

TYNDALE HOUSE PUBLISHERS
Wheaton, Illinois

Coverdale House Publishers Ltd.
London, England

Library of Congress Catalog Card Number 73-81004
ISBN 8423-0691-9 cloth; 8423-0690-0 paper

Copyright © 1973 Tyndale House Publishers, Wheaton, Illinois

Second printing, October 1973

Printed in the United States of America

With gratitude to my wife, Myrna.

How many writers are
married to their editor?

and like it!

Contents

Introduction 11

Prologue 15

1 / No Rules 27

2 / Satan's Sermon 35

3 / Aunt Grace and the Gang 43

4 / My Brother's Keeper 55

5 / Round Two, Round Three, Round 65

6 / Countdown 75

7 / "I Told You I'd Be Back" 89

8 / It's His Battle 97

Introduction

SHADOWY BUT REAL A few days ago, I took a quick look at the magazine rack at our local supermarket checkout counter. Suddenly, the occult became very much alive. There was a practical guide on how to improve your luck, and one on a simplified way to tell your fortune with cards. A guide to the mysteries of numerology was next to a complete set of horoscopes for the year, and another on the secrets of the tarot.

What these booklets had in common was an enticing appeal to exercise unnatural, or supernatural, powers over life and people. And, in spite of the fact that they were dealing with out-of-the-ordinary power, they did not involve the God of historic Judeo-Christianity.

The old cry from church pulpits against materialism still strikes home, but many sophisticated moderns know the emptiness of that route. They are interested in power, but no longer the power that comes from wealth. Social commentators on our times tell us that this is quickly becoming the age of the "supernatural." Witchcraft and Satan worship are not only commonplace today but accepted by many people. Kids play with séances, magic writing, astroprojection. The drug scene is described as deeply religious, because it opens the user to other-than-natural experiences. An acquaintance of mine — once a professing Christian — told me not too long ago, "With this mystic (drug) experience, I have *more* than Jesus Christ!"

There are many good Christian books available on the biblical assessment of demon activity. This book is not primarily a theological discussion, nor is it intended to be a shocker. But, because of its subject matter, it contains elements of both. This is a narrative, a story that really happened. You will live through one frightening week in the lives of a young couple as they came face-to-face with the adversary of their souls.

This account will raise some theological questions, such as the possibility of Christians being occupied by demons. The story will not settle such questions, but it may add some light to further understanding of this important matter.

Obviously, for protective reasons, all names and places have been changed. But it is, nonetheless, a true story. The events covered happened over a period of a little more than a year. After giving necessary background in a Prologue, most of the book concentrates on one week in which the heart of the struggle is revealed. My material came to me first-person, and I have related it the way it came.

It is the dilemma of man that evil, while repelling, is at the same time compelling, fascinating. C. S. Lewis, in *That Hideous Strength,* puts it this way: "It is idle to point out to the perverted man the horror of his perversion: while the fierce fit is on, that horror is the very spice of his craving. It is ugliness itself that becomes, in the end, the goal of his lechery."

A discussion of the power of God often meets with "hohums," but a discussion on the power of Satan usually attracts a ready audience. This fact alone helps document our tragically fallen state. (Why, for instance, have you picked up this book?)

In writing this account, I intend that God's real power be seen for what it is. Certainly, you will see the craftiness of Satan. You will see him take merciless advantage of those in his power. His basic purpose, as many scholars of demonism have pointed out, is the eternal destruction of his subjects. Satan is the enemy even of those he favors with his power.

But as devious, relentless, cruel, and destructive as he is, Satan has no power against our Lord Jesus Christ. That was proved in their face-to-face confrontation in the Gospels, and continues to be proven in open combat today. If, when the reader has finished this book, he is left with more of an impression of Satan's power than of God's, then I unintentionally have been the devil's accomplice; I pray that this will not be the case.

We Christians are all involved in real warfare. If you hesitate to believe it, come in and see *The Enemy* in action — and in defeat.

Jim Grant
Wheaton, Illinois

13

Prologue

1. THE BROTHERS Someone has said that an avalanche starts under the snow with little unseen cracks in the ice. I guess we know something about that.

My wife Betsy and I had heard of the brothers long before we met them. They were represented as neighborhood "characters" to be feared and avoided at all costs. But when they walked by the house, they didn't look as threatening as we'd expected; just a couple of tall, blond, teen-aged boys, a little rough around the edges, perhaps, but with rugged good looks and ready smiles. And when the few chances to say "Hi," and chat a little came up, the brothers seemed as ordinary as any of the boys who were showing up for our Bible study and club meetings. If anything, the brothers were quieter and more respectful than some of the other kids.

The first contact with any substance to it came one Saturday morning as we were gathering neighborhood teens together for games and Bible study. The brothers happened along the street just as we were getting the last of the stragglers into the house. At first, I mistook them for a couple of late arrivals, but Betsy set me straight. "They're not in the club, Tim," she whispered. "That's Bob and Jack Trammel."

Of course, by that time I'd slowed up enough to recognize them myself. "So?" I said. "If what we hear is true, they need the Lord more than most of the kids in there." I called to them, "Why don't you fellas look in on what's happening here this morning? You might like it!"

Well, you'd have thought I'd thrown a live grenade in the air! The brothers just stopped, then turned and walked up the driveway toward the house. But inside the house a roar of protest went up. "If they come in, we leave!" "Don't let 'em near here. They'll steal you blind!"

Now, I heard these things from out in the yard, so I knew Bob and Jack did, too. And I was embarrassed. A number of the kids in our club were Christians and should have known better than to scare off possible converts. But the brothers didn't seem to mind the response as much as I did. If I remember correctly, they sort of looked at each other with slight smiles, and then looked in the door.

They were standing in the doorway, so I had to squeeze through. I was overly apologetic as I entered the living room because of the now quieting uproar. That morning, we might as well have forgotten the meeting. The brothers stood in the doorway and watched, and their very presence subdued all spontaneity and enthusiasm. The club kids kept shooting fearful glances toward the door, and no one concentrated. I remember thinking when it was over that we could forget Bob and Jack as potential club members. They couldn't have been interested in the lifeless show they'd just watched.

That morning set Betsy and me thinking. Why should these two brothers have the neighborhood so thoroughly frightened? They weren't that much bigger or tougher-looking than other boys their age. All we really had to go on was the kids' insistence: "They're meaner than anybody."

We began hearing stories of how these brothers would catch live animals and torture them to death; how they would break into homes, stores, even the school, and demolish everything that wasn't nailed down; how they would terrorize anyone their age or younger whom they happened to find alone. Frankly, I thought some of the stories were exaggerated. And besides, Christians are in the healing business; right? We are to move into hostile situations with the love of Jesus Christ and redeem them. I say this with a tremor now, because, although I still believe it totally, I had no idea then what it might mean.

The Lord brought these boys to Betsy's and my mind over and over in the weeks following that first Saturday. We knew that the brothers had no friends, no one to whom they could talk. And we'd heard rumors, here and there, about a pretty terrible home situation. It seemed to us that we were called to bring these boys into the family of God, through Jesus Christ. And we set about to obey that call.

We had learned better than to invite them into situations where there were other kids who knew them. That had been disastrous. So we began inviting them to our home anytime we saw them. Sometimes we shared a coke and rapped. Sometimes we played chess; Bob was pretty good, and he had frightened off all available local opponents.

It was during a chess game one evening that he did a strange thing. I was beating him, if you can say that about a close chess game, and suddenly he bowed his head and seemed to pray.

"Did you just ask God to help you?" I asked, smiling. My smile reflected a sense of delight that he might be responding to some of our conversations.

"No," he answered quickly. His answer was sharply defensive. Then he relaxed into a smug smile. "I don't need God. My Thirteen Guardians help me when I need them."

I should have taken him seriously. But at the time I saw it as some kind of childish carryover from Hansel and Gretel. I also saw it as an opportunity for witness. "All

17

right," I came back at him. "I guess I'd better pray to my Lord, and ask him to help me. We'll see what happens."

I did, and in four moves I had checked him. He was greatly impressed, and I felt a small victory for "our side."

During times like that, the bits and pieces of their lives began coming together for us. We found that their home life was anything but healthy. Their father, an ex-convict who had served many years for many crimes, lived in St. Louis. Their mother had divorced him when the boys were five and six and had married again.

If she had hoped to provide a father-figure for the brothers, she had failed. The stepfather, Pete Trammel, was tough with the boys. Instead of disciplining, he attacked them when they got in his way. His punishments ran from beatings with a garden hose to confinement in their locked room for days at a time.

The brothers obviously hated him and grew up counting the days until they were bigger than he was. When they were finally large enough to fight him, the man began to sleep with a thirty-eight caliber revolver under his pillow. He announced, "If either of you come out of your room after eleven o'clock at night, I'll kill you!"

As this picture began to take shape, we understood why, above all the crimes on the boys' lengthening records at the police station, running away topped the list. And we were even more convinced that these boys *had* to know God's love. But when our conversation came around to the topic of love they simply had no understanding of the word. We might as well have been trying to communicate with two members of a remote pagan tribe.

Angela, the brothers' mother, was as crude as the man she had married. A tousled blonde in rumpled clothes, she spiked her language with vulgarities, and she made no attempt to explain away her many "boyfriends." And yet, in some mysterious way, the brothers revered their mother. When she asked them for something, they generally gave her what she wanted. When she expressed an opinion, it wasn't long before it was also their opinion. This was especially distressing to us when she decided that we were doing her boys more harm than good. Only through much prayer and cajoling were we able to maintain contact.

Betsy and I began daydreaming of the tremendous effect on the neighborhood when finally we were able to bring these boys to Jesus Christ. We saw ourselves in assorted victorious poses, most of them humble, of course, as the boys gave their testimonies at some large meeting. Looking back now, I see that the Lord had a great deal of work to do on *us*.

After a few months of casual meetings, Bob and Jack began to open up about their lives and their feelings. And they began allowing our interest to intrude on their activities. We would look at their problems from a scriptural perspective and pray with them. Bob and Jack never prayed, but they tolerated our prayers and sometimes seemed grateful for our concern.

But something began to happen; they noticed the development before we did. It seemed that every time they became impressed with the touch of the Lord on their lives, and they expressed a slight interest in his ways, something disrupting struck them.

Once when spiritual progress was becoming evident, Angela decided her growing sons and their burgeoning independence were infringing on her "private life." She decided to have them committed to a detention home on the basis of past crimes. That notion passed, but other times they were simply kicked out and had to sleep where they could. In every case we prayed, and our merciful Lord changed attitudes and circumstances. Often the problem itself became a way of showing God's power.

There were weeks when we didn't see Bob or Jack at all. We believed it was because of pressures at home to stay away, and we tried to be patient. If we could have done it legally, we would have charged into the Trammel home and "rescued" the boys. But the laws protect the guilty as well as the innocent when no criminal charges are established. We could only pray and help as we had opportunity.

At one point both boys came so close to trusting Jesus Christ that it made us tingle. "Tomorrow," Betsy and I assured each other, "they'll actually do it!" We were exuberant at the prospect.

But tomorrow turned out to have its own surprise. "We're goin' to St. Louis," Bob announced as they sauntered into our kitchen. "Goin' to live with relatives." And before long the whole story was out on the table. Angela was planning to leave Pete, as she'd met "the real thing," and the brothers were going to be sent away together. It was "the boys' fault" that things didn't work out with Pete, she rationalized, and she wasn't about to let that happen with her new man. She had bought them train tickets and given them a few dollars. Her plan was painfully simple: they were to go to relatives in St. Louis and say they had run away because Pete was cruel to them.

We couldn't understand why they'd agreed to a thing like that, but their intense emotional tie to their mother insured their compliance.

We also couldn't understand why the Lord would let such a thing happen at that time. The brothers had seemed ready, just the day before, to make a commitment to Christ, and now they might be leaving us forever. During this time the invisible spiritual conflict began to become more apparent. Every time some progress was made in the direction of their salvation, a major setback or problem arose. The brothers saw it as a simple one-to-one relationship: "Get near religion, and you get trouble." We saw it as the work of the devil, and the picture was coming into somber focus.

Surprisingly, the brothers were back within a few weeks. The brothers had told their relatives what actually happened and an angry uncle had gone to the police. The plan had failed.

We were about to "cheer" because of the way God handled the situation when it became complicated. Since the brothers had a long history of running away, the police believed Angela's story that the boys were truant. Before the dust settled on this, we saw the Lord change attitudes in the juvenile officials and the court. The brothers were eventually cleared of running away, but by then the subject of Jesus Christ had faded from their minds. When we got together with them again, Betsy and I had to begin all over in leading them back toward the Lord.

It constantly surprised us that as often as we had to start over it never got easier. In fact, at times it seemed that the brothers tuned us out when we got close to facing Jesus' offer of salvation. Once in a while, one would become suddenly, violently ill, and getting him settled and feeling better completely derailed our effort to confront them with our Lord.

This was the way our relationship fluctuated for the next two years. Bob and Jack would glimpse a reality and life in our God. At times they would even call on him for help in a bad situation. And every time he helped. He changed people and situations, showing Bob and Jack that he was near. And they almost surrendered to him.

But while they acknowledged that something must be responding to our pleas, they saw no need in pursuing whoever or whatever it was when things settled down for them. Jack was satisfied that his wits could carry him through anything, and Bob said that he had his Thirteen Guardians.

And we didn't realize that more and more of our time, our energy, and our center of attention was focused on the brothers — the initial impulse to help was beginning to control us.

2. THE SPIRITS In the summer of 1970, Betsy and I went to a youth convention in a neighboring state, and it was as though we were suddenly set free for the first time in two years. For a whole week, we wouldn't have to react to the brothers and their problems. As we drove to the convention, we discussed how many things we had let slide in our personal lives in order to be available to Bob and Jack. We were almost giddy about be-

21

ing free from them for even a short time, and then we realized that we had been talking about them the whole way to the convention!

Betsy and I arrived at the campgrounds determined that we would not even mention the names of the brothers, let alone talk about them. We knew discussion of them could be fascinating to others and could occupy time that might be better spent in pondering over God's Word and will for us. I believe it was the Lord himself who made us aware of this danger.

For the first day we really basked! We just relaxed in the woodsy atmosphere, took long walks, watched birds, and praised God for the chance to breathe clean, serene air. It was wonderful to see Betsy running like a little girl along forest paths, looking more untroubled than she had in a long time. And I actually climbed a tree! There was that same atmosphere we enjoyed during courtship: freedom, fun, love. I suppose some people at the conference had real questions about our spiritual state. But our Lord knew we needed a physical release as much as anything, and that first night we slept more soundly than we had for nearly two years.

We thanked God for the "Rest and Recreation." It's ironic that we used that term, "R & R," not knowing we were about to go into a battle which would tax every bit of physical, mental, emotional, and spiritual strength we could muster.

In the cabin next to ours was a young couple, also in youth work, Bill and Marge Gibson. We hit it off quickly, and before long we were all laughing at escapist remarks such as, "Good to get away for a while," and others that peppered our conversations. We seemed to sense mutual pressures in our work, and in spite of our resolutions Betsy and I soon were sharing what we were "escaping" from. Over coffee, in twilight walks, and at meal times we told the Gibsons about the brothers, and the Gibsons unfolded their situation to us.

Nothing in our experience had prepared us for the Gibsons' strange revelations. Betsy and I believed that Christians are involved in a battle with the enemy of our souls, Satan. We could see some of the hindrances the devil threw into our work with the brothers. But when it came to matters of demon possession or supernatural acts of satanic strength, I wasn't ready to believe those. I think I believed in Satan the way a lot of people "believe" casually in God — as some curious power that you didn't need to pay attention to because he isn't very interested in you.

As a Christian, I had gone through Bible studies on the devil and his purposes and powers, much as I had done in regard to the Holy Spirit and his Person and ministry. I'm afraid the scriptural teachings about the devil and about the indwelling power of the Spirit of Jesus Christ did not make it past my mind to my own spirit. This, I now realize, is exactly what the evil Adversary wants: ignore him so he can destroy unobserved.

Bill and Marge Gibson were church youth leaders in a large, sophisticated, evangelical congregation. A well-educated and attractive couple, they were not prone to emotionalism, but what they shared with us almost made Betsy and me question their mental stability.

They claimed they had talked with and cast out demons from people in their prosperous church. A number of Christian people had been freed from illness and strange attacks, and Bill and Marge were used by the Lord to do it. They related case after case of people in their church or community who had been possessed by demons that audibly identified themselves. Wild, erratic behavior frequently characterized the people under the control of evil spirits, and the Gibsons quietly told of the violent way in which these evil spirits fled from the power of Jesus Christ.

Betsy and I were skeptical about demons influencing modern Americans, but Bill and Marge weren't arguing theories about demons. No matter how I tried to shift the explanation to psychological or emotional causes, Bill was ready with another first-hand story which deflated my argument.

"Believe me, Tim," he said repeatedly, "I know how you

feel about this. I was the same way. But check out the Scriptures. It was true then, and it's true now."

It turned out that the four of us spent most of our spare time that week going through the Scriptures. We read of demons speaking to Jesus and with the apostles, trying to destroy their victims, massing in great numbers, residing in humans, and panicking and fleeing before the power of Jesus Christ. A verse that broke through to me was Mark 16: 17, where Jesus promises, "And those who believe shall use my authority to cast out demons. . . ."

When Betsy and I were finally ready to admit the activity of demons in our generation, Bill revealed the reason for their sharing all this. "Tim, I think you are face to face with this same thing back at your home. I think at least one of those two brothers is being used, probably possessed, by evil spirits; I don't believe his Thirteen Guardians are imagination. And I think the Lord put us together this week so that you would know what you are up against back there."

The Gibsons were sensitive enough to know when to leave us alone with our thoughts and our Lord. Betsy and I sat in our cabin for long periods of time, not speaking. Then we would share a phrase of Scripture, and pray.

From Ephesians: "Your strength must come from the Lord's mighty power within you. Put on all of God's armor so that you will be able to stand safe against all strategies and tricks of Satan. For we are not fighting against people made of flesh and blood, but against persons without bodies — the evil rulers of the unseen world, those mighty satanic beings and great evil princes of darkness who rule this world; and against huge numbers of wicked spirits in the spirit world."

From 2 Corinthians: "If the good news we preach is hidden to anyone, it is hidden from the one who is on the road to eternal death. Satan, who is the god of this evil world, has made him blind, unable to see the glorious light of the gospel that is shining upon him, or to understand the amazing message we preach about the glory of Christ, who is God."

From 1 Peter: "Be careful — watch out for attacks from

Satan, your great enemy. He prowls around like a hungry, roaring lion, looking for some victim to tear apart. Stand firm when he attacks. Trust the Lord; and remember that other Christians all around the world are going through these sufferings, too."

We read the Gospel of Mark together, and were shocked to see incident after incident of demon possession that we'd easily slipped over in the past. We prayed a lot for stability in our responses. I think I was still looking for explanations other than the supernatural for our two young "friends" back home. If I'd had a choice between going back and wrestling with "principalities and powers," or simply outlasting the social and psychological barriers between the souls of the brothers and the calling of Jesus Christ, I would have gladly chosen the second, no matter how many years it might take.

But there was finally no choice. We were only human beings, and this was a battle involving powers we had never understood as being *our* enemies.

That last morning, we said a quiet farewell and thank you to the Gibsons, shared a short prayer, and started for home with mixed feelings. The devil had been undermining us for nearly two years; now we were going home at least aware of who our enemy was.

1

No Rules

"The place is a madhouse! All they do is argue and fight with each other!"

We were listening to Jesse Anderson, a young man who had been a tremendous help to us in our work with young people, and who had recently taken a strong liking to the brothers. While we had been away, Jesse had spent time praying and listening to the brothers, and somehow he had managed to convince Angie and Pete to take him into the Trammel home as a paying boarder! When Jesse had suggested moving in, we had thought it a good one. Now we weren't so sure.

"First couple of days," Jesse was telling us, "I spent a lot of time talking about the things of God and reading the Bible and praying with Bob and Jack. But — I don't know —

it's funny — I never knew whether they were really listening."

I suppose Betsy and I exchanged a look at that point, because Jesse asked, "What do you know that I don't?"

"Please, go on," Betsy said, not really answering his question. "Tell us all about your stay there."

"Well, there's not a whole lot to say. We started out just great, and then — well, you might say that hell broke loose."

"Like what?"

"Well, right in the middle of a good discussion their mother would come into the room. She'd just walk right into their bedroom; not even knock. She must have been listening outside the door because she would pick up the conversation and mess it all up. I never met anybody who hates God more than she does, and she sure lets you know where she stands."

"Does this happen all the time?"

"If it isn't that, it's something else. Nutty things, like just about the time I think we're getting somewhere, one of the brothers gets a phone call. Or one time a chair Jack was sitting on broke apart; sent him sprawling. It completely shattered the talk we were having. I know it sounds crazy, but it's like there are all kinds of things you can't see resisting your saying anything good about God. I don't know — it was like a hundred coincidences, or maybe *planned* accidents."

Jesse was young, and a fairly new Christian, but he was sharp. We had known him first as a tragic figure. He had dropped out of a nearby university and had wandered around in the dull haze of the drug scene. One of the Lord's "planned accidents" had brought us together. I had picked him up as a hitchhiker one hot summer afternoon. The air conditioning in my car had held him long enough for me to get through what I had to say about Jesus Christ, forgiveness, and an abundant life. We parted, but a few weeks later he phoned. And a few hours later he visited us. After several more conversations he gave his life into the loving hands of the Savior.

Since Jesse's Christian walk began, our God had totally

cleansed him of the desires and hang-ups that had kept him fogged in. He had more than once shown real power in witnessing and helping some who were caught in his old traps.

After we told Jesse all that we'd been learning the last few days, our subdued co-worker said, "Maybe it's not such a hot idea for me to stay there."

"That's exactly what I was thinking, friend," I said. "It looks like we're up against powers that we don't know much about."

We prayed. It was the kind of prayer we were going to find ourselves praying more and more. It was a prayer of helplessness that says, "Lord, I just don't know what to do. This is beyond me. But, Lord, it isn't beyond you."

Then Jesse left for the brothers' home to collect his belongings. I asked if he'd like me to go along, but he said he could handle it. "Uhh, you might pray for me," Jesse said as he left, with one of those smiles that says, "I'm really more serious than I'd like to let on."

And we did. Betsy and I prayed that the Lord would ward off any evil thing that might want to harm him or impede his leaving. We asked God to cast out the spirits that might be waiting for him in that house.

About forty-five minutes later, Jesse called to say that he was moving in with a friend, and that all went well. We began to thank the Lord for the way things went when the phone rang again.

"You did it! You're responsible for this, and we'll get you for it!" Even though he was shouting and his voice distorted, I recognized Bob. "We'll get you for it! We'll *all* get you for it."

"Take it easy, Bob," I said soothingly. "There's no need to get upset. Jesse hasn't . . ."

"You better stay inside," he interrupted, "because you aren't safe outside anymore!" Then he hung up. That was the first time I'd heard the anger and hatred I'd been told about. And, frankly, it was frightening.

"Who was that, sweetheart?" Betsy called from the other room.

I tried to make light of it. I did an imitation of one of those old-time stage villains, and twirled an imaginary mustache, but wives are hard to fool.

"What if it wasn't even Bob doing the talking?" she asked quietly.

Before that evening ended, we both had a chance to listen carefully to that voice. Bob called twice more, and both calls were filled with cursing and threats against God, Jesse, Betsy, and me. He kept saying, "We'll *all* get you!" When I asked him what that meant, he just said, "You know," and went into a string of threats.

Need I say we didn't sleep well that night? And when we were awake, we were praying.

"I'd say there was a good chance you were actually talking to Bob's demon," Marge Gibson was talking to Betsy on the phone. "If he was that irrational, and used some of that language aimed at God, I'd say that's who he was."

"But can a demon just take over like that? I mean, there was no reason to be that upset. I'd think the demon would be happy for Jesse to go. Aren't there any rules?"

"Oh, Betsy, I wish we lived closer. It isn't *what* rules, it's *who* rules that matters. There aren't any rules. None at all. Jesse's leaving was probably upsetting to Bob for good reasons, but that's all his spirit companion needed to leap in and have a field day. Of course, it doesn't make much sense. In fact, that's one of the things to look for in demons: total lack of logic. Sometimes they come on as almost straight emotion: hatred, lust, confusion."

"I feel so sorry for Bob."

"That's good. Chances are, when he's more himself, he'll come by to see you. And he *may not even know* he made those calls!"

As it turned out, Marge was right about Bob's coming by. He was at the door about noon, much as in past days when it looked as though we were his only chance for a good lunch. I wasn't home, and Betsy was frightened. But Betsy is also a good trouper.

"Would you like a little lunch? Tim isn't here . . ." and then she added quickly, "but I expect him any minute."

Bob sat down at the kitchen table casually. "I guess you heard."

"Heard what?"

"Jesse moved out last night. Guess he couldn't take it."

"Couldn't take it?"

"Really made me mad. I like Jesse."

"What — uh — what did you do when Jesse left?"

"Nothing. Just sat around. Went to bed."

"You don't remember . . ."

"Huh?"

"Nothing."

The rest of the lunch went on normally. Bob asked how our trip was, how I was, and when he could stop by and talk with me again. Betsy said, "Anytime." And that was that.

As Bob was going out the door he said, "I like talking with Tim. Aunt Grace doesn't like it, but I think he's all right." And he was gone before Betsy could' even begin a further question.

I have to admit that I found it difficult to accept the idea that Bob didn't know anything about the calls he had made the night before. I had *heard* him. I *knew* his voice, and although I believed more in the power of evil spirits than I had a few weeks earlier, there were pretty big gaps in that conviction.

I think Betsy sensed that I wasn't entirely convinced about Bob's story, so she switched the subject to what he had said on his way out. Did I know who Aunt Grace was? Why didn't *she* like me? Until today, we'd never heard her name mentioned.

A check by phone with Jesse didn't help at all. He'd never heard her name mentioned by any member of the Trammel family.

And so we were again praying that prayer that says, "Lord, what's going on?" It's a temptation to use hindsight at this point and call attention to what we didn't realize ourselves then. We were getting more and more involved in solving the mystery of the brothers, and less involved in bringing them to the Lord. What is there about evil that is attractive — even when you're trying to battle it?

Our mounting phone bill was an additional problem as we talked frequently with our confidants, the Gibsons.

"Check it out, Tim," Bill told me. And when he said that, I knew he had already checked it as thoroughly as I would. "Nowhere in the Bible are we told to ask God to cast out demons. We're told over and over that he has *already triumphed* over evil, so to ask him to do it again would be useless."

"But people *do* seem to cast out spirits," I protested.

"That's just the point. *People* do. Over and over we're told in the Bible that the followers of Jesus Christ will do the casting out, will show the same miraculous actions that he exhibited when he walked the earth. Check the last few verses in Mark. Or read John 14 again, carefully. Or check through Acts; see for yourself what his followers *did* as well as what they said."

I *could* have hit Bill with something like, "Where is all that power today? Where is the healing, the miracles, the casting out?" But his answer would have been: "Right here." How do you argue about the power of the Holy Spirit with a guy who is a channel for that power? But I couldn't buy it — at least not yet.

"You see, you have to remember that these spirits are every bit as much the creation of God as you are. Only they willfully went wrong. God cast them out of heaven. Now, there are all kinds of theories as to how these fallen spirits became attached to this earth. The Bible doesn't spend a lot of time on them. But it does make clear that they are bad news, and equally clear that, because of the power of Jesus Christ, his life, his death, and his resurrection, these powers are conquered. Jesus said, 'I have been given *all* authority in heaven and earth,' and, Tim, if that isn't enough . . .'"

"I understand."

"I'm telling you this, Tim, because I think you're in for something, now that they know you're on to them."

"They know?"

"They're not stupid. And they don't like to have their bodies discovered."

"Their bodies?"

"That's something that seems pretty constant. Remember when Jesus cast out the legion? They asked for other bodies, rather than being sent to some sort of torment. That's when Jesus cast them into the herd of pigs."

"And the pigs ran into the river and drowned."

"Right. Anyway, they seem to *need* bodies. It's either that, or something torturous. Look at Luke 8:31. And when they're discovered, they don't leave happily. You'll see."

At the time, I wished he hadn't added, "You'll see." I still wish he hadn't. But he did. And he was right.

This night, we actually prayed for sleep. And we slept.

2

Satan's Sermon

"Can I come in?"

It was Bob at the back door again, and again at lunch time. Betsy was alone.

"I should have expected it," Betsy thought whimsically, but her voice said gently, "Come in, Bob. Like a little lunch?"

"Okay."

"He was almost totally silent the whole time he was here," Betsy told me when I returned home that afternoon. "It was like he wanted to talk, but . . . I don't know."

"Well, let's find out," I said, reaching for the phone.

"Hello?"

"Bob?"

"Yeah."

"This is Tim. How are you?"

"Okay."

The first of many long pauses followed.

"Uh, Betsy thought you might like to talk for a while."

"Yeah."

"We've got some time tonight, if you'd like."

A long pause, and then it occurred to me that we weren't available. "I'm sorry, Bob. I just remembered we're committed tonight."

"Okay."

"Maybe you'd like to come along. We're going to a teen prayer meeting. You might like to see what the Lord is doing in the lives of other kids. What do you say?"

"I don't think so."

"Why not give it a try? Listen to what kids your own age have to say about how he walks with them. We'd *love* to have you come along." A quick look at Betsy showed me she immediately forgave my stretch of the truth. "We could talk the whole way there and back, and it won't run too late. What do you say?"

This time I expected the pause.

"Bob? What do you say. Will you come with us?"

"Okay."

"Terrific! We'll pick you up at about a quarter of seven. Don't forget, now."

"I'll be ready."

"Man, I hope something gets through to him." Jesse was pacing back and forth in our living room as Betsy added the finishing touches to her hair, and I made sure the back door was locked.

"So do I. I hope *Someone* gets through," I said.

Betsy came from the bathroom. "Do you think we ought to call him just to be sure?"

I thought that was a good idea, and did it. Bob said he was all ready to go, and even sounded more anxious about it than I'd expected. So Jesse, Betsy, and I hopped into the car and headed toward the Trammel home.

"He didn't say nothin' about it," Jack said, when I asked

him if Bob was ready to go. "He went with Pete to pick up a paycheck. They just left. Where you goin', anyhow?"

"To a prayer meeting."

Jack smiled. "And you think Bob would go with you?"

"He said he would."

"Well, he isn't here. You figure it out."

Back in the car, we had some retrenching to do. I backed out of the driveway slowly and headed up the street.

"That's really strange," Betsy said. "Bob never goes anywhere with his stepfather."

"That's what I was thinking," added Jesse. "Man, they hate each other. They never do anything together but fight."

"Then why . . . ?" I never had to finish the question. Of course! It was simple. Bill had warned me that when demons know you're on to them, they'll hide out. With a kind of sickening pity, I pictured the two belligerents: Bob in his late teens, carrying around an evil presence which did little but torture him and cause him trouble; and Pete, older, with his own inner adversary. When things were going "normally," the demons had them pick and fight at each other. But when help approached, the demons needed these two to be friends and the conflict stopped. This was my first close look at the evilness of evil. And it was probably my first really sympathetic look at Bob.

I pulled the car into another driveway and turned around.

"What are you doing?" Betsy sometimes sounds as uncertain about her husband as other wives I've heard about.

"Staying," I said. "To run now is to give the devil what he wants. That poor kid needs help, and we're going to wait until he gets back."

"But what about the prayer meeting?"

"The place will be crawling with Christians. As far as I can see, we're the only Christians here." That seemed to settle things. I brought the car to a stop across the street and a few houses away from the Trammel home. And we sat and waited.

It seemed a lot longer, but in about half an hour we saw the Trammel car pull into the driveway and Pete and Bob get out. I was out and over there before they reached the front door.

"Set to go, Bob?" I asked, trying to sound as casual as my pounding heart would allow. For the first time I felt I was actually facing something evil and powerful, and that these two figures in front of me were merely containers. I don't mind saying I was frightened, and that my mind kept saying, "Lord, Lord, Lord" as I stood there.

"Where you goin'?" Pete asked suspiciously.

"Bob said he'd like to go to a meeting with us," I answered for him.

"Well, now he *wouldn't* like to," Pete also answered for him. "We got a few things we're goin' to do together, my-uh-son and me."

This was almost too much! "We won't be late," I said. I knew that was lame, but I wasn't used to this kind of battle.

"Don't let 'em make you do anything you don't want to, Bobby, boy," Pete said, slapping Bob on the back. "You want to sit around with a bunch of religious nuts, or how about that little ride we were talking about?"

"I really think you'd get a lot, personally, out of this meeting, Bob," I tried. And at the same time, I prayed. "O Lord, what can I say to make this meeting at least as appealing to Bob as his stepfather's plans? I'm really out of my league, Lord. Please . . ."

Pete's voice broke into my consciousness. He was repeating what I'd just said, with a sing-song mock. ". . . a lot, personally, out of this meeting, Bob." And then he laughed.

"Would you shut up out there!" Angie had heard the discussion. "What's going on, anyway?"

"The preacher-man is here to take Bobby off and save his soul!" Pete sang out. Angie appeared at the door. "Well, isn't that nice," she smiled. Then her expression hardened. "Look, fella, I've got enough problems without you turning my boys against me. That religion stuff is for soft-heads, and my boys aren't soft! Now, come on in here, Bobby, and tell that friend of yours to go whistle."

"Don't let them make you do anything you don't want to, Bob," I heard myself say. Those were the same words Pete had used just a little earlier! "Oh, no," I thought. "Lord, you sure have the wrong man on this job."

Bob hadn't said a word the whole time. Now it was only a quick, quiet sentence. "I'll be back later," he stated, and walked toward our car. I stumbled along, following, hardly believing what I was seeing.

There were loud protests from the house but he walked straight to the car, got in, and I drove off a little faster than I might have otherwise.

"As you can see, Bob, everyone here believes in the supernatural. Why don't you share some of your experiences? I know everyone would be interested in what you have to say." There I was, sticking my neck out again, but it seemed the right thing to do at the meeting.

Bob had just listened to a dozen young people tell how Jesus Christ had moved into their lives and completely changed them. Some had been playing with drugs, some with the occult, some with nothing at all. But Jesus had come, and been invited in, and these kids were radiant with what abundant life was all about. Bob had listened with his customary vague expression. I had no idea what he'd come out with.

He shifted in his chair, cleared his throat, and then said simply, "I don't want to talk about it now."

There was a small flurry of encouragement from the others. Bob again shifted, and then said, "Well, I believe in the Lord."

A few pleased smiles broke out among the young people, but Jesse, Betsy, and I must have looked like someone threw cold water in our faces! He believed in the Lord? What a thing for Bob Trammel to come up with! "Lord, what's going on?" was in the air again.

I couldn't let it rest. "Uh, Bob, it seems to me that when we've talked before, you've said things like you didn't need Jesus Christ because you had your Thirteen Guardians. Has that changed?"

39

Bob was starting to breathe at a staccato rate. "Look, I'm just sitting here, minding my own business, and I see that all of you people believe in — in the Lord, and I don't want to cause any trouble, so I decided to go along with you. This way I won't offend anybody, see?"

The pleased smiles had faded as soon as the tone of his voice told us where he was emotionally. Now all attention was focused on Bob, and he didn't seem to like it.

"Just tell us what you *do* believe, Bob," I said quietly. "Tell us the truth."

"You wouldn't believe the truth if you heard it," he said, so quietly it seemed he almost spoke to himself.

"Try us."

Bob sat still a long time, the only sound in the room being his forced breathing. There were large drops of perspiration forming on his forehead. Finally he brought a sleeve up to dry his face, and he began talking. There was an air of confidence in his speech that I'd never heard before. It was as though he was reciting a practiced speech; not as though he were reading, exactly, but as though it was all ordered and lined up for his delivery.

"All right. You talk about your Lord. You talk about your God of love, and all that. Where do you get all the stuff you talk about? From that Bible, right? From a book nobody knows for sure was really written by the God you all talk about. Me, I get my ideas and my beliefs direct. My guardians don't just get me out of jams. They tell me things, things that are going to happen, things that make sense out of life.

"They tell me that all this stuff about your Lord and love is all crap! They show me how everything everybody does is what they are *destined* to do. If you are the kinda guy who is loving, it's because you are *destined* to be. If I'm not, I'm not *destined* to be. Everybody is already doing what they were meant to do, and it's nuts to think you change anything. You can't change destiny."

There was a shocked stillness in the room, as we all began to realize what he was saying. One boy hesitantly ventured a comment, "But Jesus Christ died to change us."

"He was *destined* to die. He even said so himself. Look what he said just about the time the priests and everybody closed in on him. He said this was the reason he came."

My mind was stuttering at this point. Here was Bob preaching to us a philosophy that certainly wasn't biblical, and using events in Scripture to make his points! How could he do that? How would he know that statement in John 12:27? Had I ever used it in one of our talks? Even so, how could his mind hang on to it?

"But if what you say is true, it doesn't really matter whether someone is a Christian or not. They're just doing what they are destined to do, no matter what they do." Betsy was summarizing his sermon almost too well!

"That's right!" Bob was animated with delight at our understanding.

I hastily interjected: "But that means if I'm a murderer — if I go around hurting people — it doesn't matter because I'm destined to do it."

"Right!"

"And if I kill you?" I stopped there, and waited. It was obvious that my question had jarred something inside him, but the shake was so slight that only those of us who knew him saw it. "Demons need bodies" — Bill's words flashed in my mind. Was that it? Were we once again listening to the demon in Bob?

Again, Bill's words came to me. "Over and over we're told in the Bible that the followers of Jesus will do the casting out." My mind was almost splitting with frustration. Should I just shout something like, "In the name of Jesus I command you to leave"? What if there really isn't a demon there? What would Bob say to that? What would the others say? They'd think I'd come unglued! And I could just imagine the conversation on the way home! I could hear myself saying lamely to Bob as I dropped him off, "Come on over anytime and chat."

And yet, there he was, preaching a totally godless philosophy to the group, and backing it up with Scripture I knew he'd never studied. I remembered the words of James where he says, "Believing in one God? Well, remember that the demons believe this too — so strongly that they tremble in terror!"

Of course, demons know the Scriptures. And they would certainly know how to misuse them! And didn't Bob say that he got his information direct? His Guardians told him what he believed!

It was obvious. The demon was there, and speaking. He should be confronted. But . . .

As I hung in indecision, a girl in the group asked Bob if he'd like to receive Jesus Christ as his Savior. I thought the question was out of place, but it was more than I was doing.

"No," was Bob's reply.

"Then would you mind if we prayed for you?"

"Why doesn't she let him go?" I thought. "Doesn't she know what she's up against?" But still *I* did nothing.

"I guess that's okay," Bob said, and again I was tossed off balance. Why should he say it was okay to pray for him? Didn't his demon know that he was in danger?

As I look back on that meeting, it was as though I was watching a drama. *I* knew what spiritual forces were at work but I didn't do much. The others didn't know what was going on, but they were showing real love and concern for Bob.

We gathered around Bob and some laid their hands on him. Then each in turn prayed briefly. Most of the prayers acknowledged that Satan was somehow involved with Bob, and asked God, through Jesus Christ, to show his power in Bob's life.

A curious feeling seemed to spread around the room. We have all since talked about it with each other. It was a warming, expanding, powerful feeling. We knew that the Holy Spirit was present with us, and that he was definitely involved in our prayers for Bob.

Nothing spectacular happened. Not at the meeting. But all of us, including Bob, left with an unusual quietness about us. Many of us were praising God in our minds, and we weren't quite sure why.

3

Aunt Grace and the Gang

"They don't even know me," Bob said as we drove home. "They don't even know me, and still they really prayed for me."

"Because they are Christians, Bob," Betsy said warmly. "Because Jesus loves you, they do too."

There was a light mist spreading across the countryside, and the headlights bored out like luminous poles and then evaporated into nothing in front of us. My mind seemed to be running to the end of the poles and back. "Just listen to him," I was saying inside. "A few minutes ago he was telling us that we were all crazy to believe Christianity, and now he's sounding like a grateful little boy because we prayed! I wish he'd stay in one place long enough to get a shot off!" As if to punctuate my thought, the headlights flashed off the eyes of an animal at the side of the road.

"It's only ten-fifteen," Betsy said. "Would you like to stop at our house for some hot chocolate before you go home?" I remember wondering why some women thought a warm stomach was the answer to everything. But the thought dissolved as Bob answered, "Yeah. I'd like that."

"Do you have an Aunt Grace?" Jesse suddenly asked. And I could feel a tingle of tension run through the car.

"Why do you ask that?" Bob said, his voice weaker than it had been a few seconds ago.

"You mentioned her once to me," Betsy explained, "and I asked Jesse who she is."

"What did I say about her?" Bob was guarded.

My neck muscles tightened a little.

"Oh, something about her not liking Tim," Betsy tried to sound light.

There was a pause, and then Bob said, "She doesn't."

"That's funny," I chimed in, also trying to sound breezy. "She's never even seen me. How can she not like me?"

"Oh, she's seen you."

"Well, that's news to me. I've never been officially introduced. Where have we bumped into each other?"

The pause was so long that I thought Bob didn't hear my question. "Bob? Where have your aunt and I met?"

"It isn't like that."

"*What* isn't like *what?* I don't understand."

Another of Bob's pauses, and then he said, "Okay. I might as well tell you the whole thing."

We were just turning the corner of our street when Bob began. Sometime during his story we pulled into our driveway and shut off the engine and the lights. I'm not sure when that was. It happened automatically, as anything mechanical does when your mind is totally fixed on something else.

"I was seven when it happened. I was staying with my two aunts, my Aunt Grace and my Aunt Ruby. I know their names are funny, but they're old ladies.

"They used to do strange things. I mean, people used to come and ask their advice about things, and they would pull out some funny looking cards, and shuffle them around, and lay them out. And then they'd give a reading. And that person usually had some big reaction to it and gave them money, and left.

"Sometimes they'd have bunches of people in. Jack and I had to play outside when that happened. So one day I said to Aunt Grace, 'What do you do in there when you make us play outside?' And she said, 'You really want to know?' And I said, 'Yeah.'

"So she said next time they have one, I could stay. And I said, 'One what?' And she said, 'Just wait, and you'll see.'

"Well, I saw, all right! A couple of days later a lot of people started arriving at the house, and Aunt Grace said, 'You sure you want to be part of this?' And, of course, I said, 'Yeah.' So I went into the room with all the others.

"And they pulled the heavy drapes, making the room pretty dark. Then my Aunt Grace waved her hands in front of my Aunt Ruby, and she got into a trance and started talking with other voices and speaking to the people in the room. Man, it was spooky, but I didn't let on it was scaring me.

"And then something really strange happened. My Aunt Grace said she was supposed to put *me* in a trance, because she has something for me. I wasn't gonna chicken out, and I said, 'Okay.' And next thing I knew I was sitting there and could see and hear everything that was going on, but I couldn't do anything about it, if you know what I mean. I felt tied to the chair, but nothing was holding me.

"Then my Aunt Grace said she was going to give me Thirteen Guardians who will stay with me all my life and protect me from getting in trouble, and tell me things nobody else can know. She said these Guardians are the spirits of thirteen of my ancestors, and she started naming them off. And I'd heard about most of them; my aunt had told me about them. She made them out to be heroes, kinda, which is funny because they were more like criminals. Some of them were hung for murder and things like that.

"And as she started naming them, they appeared! Right

there in front of me, they showed up, and they smiled at me and then faded away.

"So ever since that time whenever I'm in a tight spot or need something special, I just call on them and they help me. They really do. And they tell me things. They show me how to have fun like nobody else has. And they . . ."

I had to break in. "Bob, wait a minute. You've got to see these Guardians for what they are. They're demons, Bob. They're evil. And all they're going to do is lead you straight into hell. Jesus said . . ."

Then it was his turn to break in. "Don't start telling me about your Lord! I've never seen your Lord. Neither have you! But I have *seen* my Guardians. You've never heard your Lord. But I have *heard* my Guardians! So don't start telling me mine are bad. If yours is so good, why doesn't he show himself?"

At some point during that outbreak Bob's attitude changed. He had started in a kind of frenzy but before he'd finished he was almost calm. His shouts had become quiet accusations. Yet in his calmness, there was a kind of driving intensity. His face was covered with perspiration, but his expression was stiff. The rest of us sitting in that car were in the presence of evil. We were face-to-face.

"We're on to you, you know," I suddenly blurted out, facing Bob. "We know you're in there, and we're going to make sure you get out!" It was frightening to face someone you know and address someone else *inside* that person.

But, inexplicably, Bob's attitude strangely changed again. He was caught up in the emotion of reliving his childhood experience and he seemed oblivious to my challenge of the demons. He went on with his story, with no response to our brief conversation. I thought the evil spirit must be teasing us in a kind of cat-and-mouse situation.

"Then, when I was older, and Aunt Grace died, something different happened. One of my Thirteen Guardians became Aunt Grace. She's the one who does most of the talking. And she's the one who still comes and visits me."

As he began to talk of the spirit of his Aunt Grace, Bob again began perspiring. His voice became shaky, and he started looking furtively out the car windows. As he finished a sentence, his emotional pitch was more tense than I'd ever seen anyone's. Betsy and Jesse began praying in the back seat.

Bob continued, "She visits me! She . . . she's *here!* She's here now! I can't see her yet but I know what it feels like when she comes! I'm really in for it now! She said never to tell you about her. She doesn't even want me to talk to you. Oh, she'll really give it to me tonight!"

He began to cry and groan, and my heart went out to this pitiful figure on the seat next to me.

"Bob, try to listen to me," I shouted in his ear. "Try to grasp what I'm saying. She can't touch us, Bob. We're safe in here. We have the protection of Almighty God. Bob, try to listen to me. You can beat her, too, if you really want to. Look at me. I'm not scared of her."

"Don't!" Bob stiffened with a frightened plea. "Don't talk about her like that! You don't know her! You don't know what she can do! You're taking a big chance, messing around with her, Tim. You really are! She'll get you, too. Leave her alone. You don't know the power she has!"

"I know the power Jesus Christ has, Bob! That's what makes the difference. He has overcome all the powers of darkness! Aunt Grace can't touch me. Look! Look at me! She can't touch me because I have the Spirit of the living Christ in me. His power, Bob! His power is supreme! Do I look scared of Aunt Grace?"

And surprisingly enough, I really wasn't. When Bob had started talking about her, I was as frightened as anyone might be in those circumstances. But as Jesse and Betsy prayed, the assurance of the power of Jesus Christ over even this bizarre situation welled up inside me, and I found myself convinced that he actually *is* superior. I don't know how many times I'd told others that "God is able," but this time I needed to know, and they were more than words. His Holy Spirit was there — in power!

"Look at yourself, Bob. Look what she's doing to you! Don't you see that you need the Lord's power in you, too?"

Bob was huddled in the car seat, looking pathetically like

photos I'd seen of mental patients. His voice was more like an animal whimper than a human sound. "She doesn't like this at all. She gets mad when I talk about the Lord. And she gets *real* mad when I come down here. Every time I come down here to see you, she comes to see me the same night. And however long I stay here, that's how long she stays with me.

"I get home and I think everything's going to be okay, and I start up the stairs and there she is! She just stands there at the top of the stairs, staring at me! Staring and staring!

"I can't stand looking at her, and I'm afraid to shut my eyes! And she's out here somewhere right now! And she'll be waiting for me when I get home! And she'll be mad!"

He finally broke into heavy sobbing. In the back seat of the car, Betsy and Jesse were crying, too, partly because of the unbearable tension, and partly in anguish for this poor boy's state.

I noticed a salty taste at the edge of my mouth, and discovered that my face had tears on it, too. But this was it. This was the confrontation that we had been prepared for, both by our conversations with the Gibsons and the prayers tonight. Little thoughts about waiting until tomorrow when we were more rested and less emotional crossed my mind, but this time I couldn't allow them. Bob was in desperate need, and he seemed to know it. This was the time to strike out against the evil forces that wanted him for themselves.

"Bob," I said, as quietly as I could, "You know what you have to do. Those Guardians are demons. They are imitating your dead relatives. Even the one you think is your Aunt Grace is a counterfeit. They want to destroy you. They want to fill your life with fear and confusion, and finally lead you straight into hell. You know that, don't you?"

I'm not sure what his answer was. He was making little frightened sounds. But I had the idea he understood.

"Look at yourself, Bob. How can anything *good* do this to you. Why would anything *good* need to keep you in fear and subjection like this? You know what I'm saying is true, don't you? You want to be free from this fear, don't you?"

Again, his only response was whimpering.

"Then listen, Bob. Listen hard. The Bible says, 'We need have no fear of someone who loves us perfectly; his perfect love for us eliminates all dread of what he might do to us.' Did you hear that, Bob. God *loves* us. He loves *you*. He can make that fear just — just evaporate! He really can. And all you need to do is ask his forgiveness and accept Jesus Christ into your heart by faith."

"I can't. I can't." He was crying like a little boy. His hands seemed to be tugging at each other as though one were on each side of his dilemma. "I want to. I can't. They won't let me."

"For God so loved the world that he gave his only begotten Son, that whosoever believeth on him should not perish but have everlasting life!" Jesse shouted the words from the back seat. He repeated it two or three times.

Bob's shirt was soaking wet. "I want to. I can't."

"The Spirit of the Lord is upon me," I quoted. "That's what Jesus said, Bob. And listen to how he continued: 'He has appointed me to preach Good News to the poor; he has sent me to announce that *captives shall be released* and the blind shall see, and that the *downtrodden shall be freed from their oppressors,* and that God is ready to give blessings to all who come to him.' You're a captive, Bob. You're oppressed. How about it? Jesus Christ wants to release you. All you have to do is say, 'Yes!'"

"She's out there listening. I can't. She'd kill me. She's going to be so mad! Please . . ."

"Try to get your mind away from her, Bob. It isn't your Aunt Grace. It's a demon, Bob. Pull yourself away and think of the Lord! The Lord, Bob! The Lord!"

"What Lord?"

We were shaken by Bob's new manner. He had stopped crying and was sitting, almost casually, leaning against the car door. He put his hands up behind his head and looked at us with a cynical little smile. And his voice was strong and clear.

"What's all this 'Lord' business about? Who needs your Lord, anyway?"

I heard a subdued, "Oh, no!" from Betsy.

He had given into the powers oppressing him and they were back in control.

"What can your Lord do that my Guardians can't? They give me everything I need. They . . ."

I was suddenly raising my voice again. This time I repeated what Bill Gibson has suggested: "In the name and power of Jesus Christ, I command you to leave this boy!"

We waited to see what would happen. Bob sat still for a second or two, then he shuddered and looked around, confused. Instantly he was back to his craven fear. "She's out there somewhere. I can feel her!"

I'm not sure which was worse to watch: his fear or his subjugation. But we knew that when he was terrified he was speaking for himself.

"Bob, try to concentrate on what I'm saying," I pleaded. "Christ Jesus came into the world to save sinners!"

"Who are you calling a sinner?" Bob replied in a strong voice again. And again we were confronting the evil spirit.

"I command you, by the name and power of Jesus Christ, to go out from him!" I said desperately.

Bob again shivered and his brow knit in confusion. This time he realized something strange was going on. "What's the matter? What just happened?"

"Bob," I said, taking his arm, "We have talked twice with the demons in you. I don't know if it's the same one, or two different ones; they use your voice, but . . ."

"They use *my* voice?" he murmured, shaken.

"You've got to listen to me while you're yourself — Jesus Christ can . . ."

"I feel strange — she's coming again! She's. . . ."

"Bob! Hang on! Jesus Christ can make you free!"

Bob just laughed, long and loud. He laughed and laughed! "Free? What do you know about freedom? What do you know about anything?"

And again I shouted, "In the name and by the power of Jesus Christ, I command you to leave him alone!"

And again Bob was quiet. "Did it happen again?" he asked.

"That's right. You are being *used,* Bob. And every time the spirits talk, I command them to leave in the name and power of Jesus Christ. And they go. Doesn't that tell you something, Bob? Doesn't that show you where the real power is? Listen to Jesse and Betsy pray. Listen to how they care for you. Don't you see, Bob? All these things you've been believing were good are actually . . ."

"I believe what I have been *shown!* I believe what is *right!*" He was again in the other's power. "Why don't you give up? Can't you see I don't need your second-hand religion when I have *first*-hand information?"

"In the name of Jesus Christ, and by the power of God over all evil, I command you to leave him alone!" I shouted. But I heard a small crack of tiredness in my voice.

"Again?" Bob looked at me wearily.

"Again." I nodded.

"O Lord Jesus," prayed Betsy, "help him to see that he needs you to be free. Help him to understand that he can be free forever from all these things that now exercise control over his body." Betsy prayed more fervently than I'd ever heard her pray. We had never taken a prayer burden as seriously as this, and so had never prayed as seriously. We were beginning to understand what dependence on God meant.

"You can be free, Bob. Have you heard me say that yet? Every time I start telling you this, you fall victim. All the Lord needs is your will, Bob. Just invite him to take over. He won't push himself. He doesn't work that way. He honors *your* will, Bob. *You* have to *want* him to help you. Can you hear me?"

"I hear you just fine," Bob answered. But his tone was as from some other conversation somewhere else. We knew he wasn't able to hear us again. Betsy and Jesse continued praying, and once again I challenged the spirit who was talking.

"In the name and power of Jesus Christ, I command you

to go!" Bob responded with a small jerk and a shake of his head.

"That's right," I answered his question before his lips formed it. I had lost count in my confusion, but my mind was putting together Bob's Thirteen Guardians with the story in Mark 5 about the man filled with many demons. Were we casting out the thirteen, one at a time? And was it necessary to get rid of them before he could actually hear that Jesus could make him permanently free? I didn't know. And I hardly had time to think. I had to play it fast and by ear, and stay with what seemed to be working.

"Jesus loves you, Bob. He wants to free you just as he has freed everyone who has come to him. He does it, Bob. Just ask him in. Let him prove to you that he is able . . ."

But it was again too late. Bob was writing with his finger on the steamy car window. He wrote, "J. C. Saves Green Stamps," and then laughed in a voice we hadn't yet heard. It was the change in voices that began to make the situation clearer to me. These must be different demons. And the ones which had spoken earlier were gone. A glimmer of hope shone in the frantic situation. If I could command them to leave one at a time, why not try all the remaining ones at once?

"In the name of Jesus Christ, and in the power of our great God, I command all you remaining evil spirits to leave this boy!" I shouted. "Now!"

Nothing happened. A quick thought raced through my mind, and I added quickly: "O Lord Jesus, protect us here in this car with your mighty power and blood!"

And with that Bob began to convulse! I've never seen anything like it and hope that I never shall again. He retched, threw himself against the dashboard and the door, screamed, scratched at the window, growled, foamed at the mouth, and finally collapsed in the seat.

For a moment we sat stunned. Then we began rolling down the car windows. The stench was almost suffocating. Bob slumped there, looking as though all the life had gone out of him. If he was breathing, it was only slightly. We stared at him in horror, not knowing what to do. Then, slowly, as one wakes from a dream, he opened his eyes and looked around. He moved and it was obvious that he was sore. He rubbed his head. He wiped his mouth and looked at his hand. His face showed that there was an unpleasant taste in his mouth. He sat up. "What happened?"

"I think," I said, my voice more shaky than I thought it would be, "I think they are gone. All of them."

"My Guardians?"

"Your demons."

He looked from me to Betsy to Jesse. We looked as though we had just survived Niagara in a barrel, and he nodded. "I think you're right," he said. "I don't feel the same. I feel — clean, somehow. I think they really *are* gone!"

"Oh, Bob, that's wonderful," Betsy said, and began crying. I think we all wept, but what a difference from just a while before when we had all cried in anguish!

But into this beautiful, emotional release the Lord intervened again and I said, "Bob, the Bible tells about a demon-possessed man who was cleansed. And after the expelled demon wandered around a while looking for a place to stay, he came back and found his old residence still empty."

"Yeah," Bob said, almost giddy with his free feeling.

"And the story goes on to say that the demon went back into the man and invited seven of his friends to go in with him."

Bob was suddenly as serious as I was. "They'll come back?" he said, some of the old fear returning to his face.

"Not if you fill *your* 'house' with God's Holy Spirit. You see, if you're empty, they'll have somewhere to live. But if you ask Jesus into your heart, he will fill all the available space, and there'll be no room for the returning demons."

"Where will they go? Where are they right now?" Bob asked, the fear still hanging there.

"I know," Jesse shouted, and reached over the seat and into Bob's shirt pocket. He pulled out Bob's well-worn aluminum cigarette case. "Let's banish them in here! And then we'll bury them!"

The relief of the venture and the feeling of being free took over, and both boys sprinted from the car into the night air.

Betsy and I followed, and soon we were all standing solemnly around a small "grave" in the garden.

"Goodbye, dear Guardians," Jesse said mockingly. "You may now guard this compost!"

We all laughed giddily, the tension of the last hour slipping away, and walked back to the house. Bob kept saying, "I'm free! I'm not afraid! I'm really free! I can feel it! Praise the Lord!"

And he kept saying it all the way home and into his front door.

At 2:30 A.M., Betsy and I collapsed into bed and sank into sleep, drenched with a consciousness of God's peace and presence and victory!

4

My Brother's Keeper

When we awoke, a bright, mid-morning sun lit the bedroom, and a phone that seemed to have been ringing many times called to us from the hall.

"Bob?" I said, gathering my thoughts, "How are you?" I was still trying to remember whether the experience of the night before had been a dream, or had really happened.

"Praise the Lord!" he sang out, and I was sure I wasn't dreaming. "I slept fine. And nobody visited me, if you know what I mean. I feel great! I'll be by later to see you."

The smile on my sleepy face must have told Betsy everything she wanted to know. "It's really wonderful, isn't it, Tim? I mean, what the Lord can do. I don't think I ever appreciated so much what we've been saved *from*."

"I know what you mean. We take our life so for granted. It's good of the Lord to keep us from seeing what's going on around us in the universe. I guess he made us with some kind of filter."

The phone rang again. This time Betsy answered. "Hello? Yes, this is . . . what? Oh, now wait a minute, Mrs. Trammel; that's not a bit true. But that's ridiculous. No. Now, look . . . uh, Mrs. Trammel, maybe you should speak to my husband. Please. No, you don't seem to understand. Will you try to let me . . . hello? Hello, Mrs. Trammel?" She replaced the receiver. "Oh, Tim! That woman makes me feel sick sometimes!"

"What's the matter?"

Betsy sat on the edge of the bed, all radiance gone. Her voice was low. "She accused me of having romantic designs on her son!"

"Bob?"

"Bob! She said that *he* said we all loved him, and she immediately translated 'love' into her street definition! Poor Bob. He tried to share with her what happened last night and she's furious. You should have heard the language she was using!"

"I've heard her explosions before."

"Oh, Tim, isn't there something we could do to get those boys away from that home? It's so painful to know what they have to face there."

"I know. But there isn't anything we can do. She's their mother. There isn't anything to do except pray. And I don't mean, 'Let's pray about it' as a cop-out."

The doorbell punctuated my words. Betsy took a deep breath. "Looks like one of us had better get dressed. Somebody told the neighborhood this is Grand Central Station!"

"Have you heard anything from Bob?" It was Jesse, and he looked a little ragged.

"He's praising the Lord," I reported with a laugh. "Talked to him just a little while ago. That whole thing last night, Jesse, really *did* happen. Come in. Sit down!"

Some of Jesse's anxiety relaxed.

"Coffee?" I asked. "We seem to have slept late."

"Man, I couldn't shut my eyes. Yeah, thanks."

Betsy was with us in a few minutes, and we recounted

the experience to each other, filling in what was going on in our minds at each step of the way. We agreed that our prayer life would never be the same again. As a matter of fact, neither would our idea of God. The experience had opened up for us what no amount of talk could ever do. We had experienced the larger forces of good and evil as actually existing and near to us. I had always smiled about anyone who would pray for protection from spirits. "Things that go 'bump' in the night," I'd think, and commend my maturity. But I knew now that I would be praying for protection.

The phone rang again, and Betsy shot a quick look at me. "You answer it, will you Tim?"

I did. "Hi, Tim, this is Jack. Hey, what's going on over there?"

"What do you mean?"

"My brother's all up in the air about something, and Mom is really upset, and they both use your name a lot. What's going on?"

"Jack, why don't you stop over, and we'll talk about it?"

As it happened, when Jack did come over I had gone to my office. Jesse had stayed to pray with Betsy about the brothers. We felt sure Jack would be easily won to the Lord now that Bob had been through this experience.

"Come in, Jack." Betsy welcomed him with more enthusiasm than usual. She and Jesse had already agreed to tell Jack the straight facts about anything he asked. And his questions came fast.

"I heard my mother cussing you out, and at the same time Bob is dancing around the house like he's some kind of TV star, smiling at everybody. . . ."

"Praise God," Jesse responded.

"What's going on?"

"Jack, sit down. Let me pour you a cup of coffee. I want you to listen very carefully to what we have to tell you." Betsy's attitude was warm and calm, but she plowed through some of the same "this-is-going-to-sound crazy" feelings that I had the night before.

Jack wound his slim, six-foot-two frame around one of the kitchen chairs, said, "Thanks," and waited.

"You remember," Betsy began, clearing her throat, even though she really didn't need to. "You remember the Guardians your brother was always talking about?"

"Sure," said Jack, sipping at the hot coffee. "He says something about them every now and again to me and Mom, but we don't believe him."

"Well, they were real."

"Huh?" Jack's coffee cup stopped midway between the table and his lips.

"Only they weren't guardians. They were demons."

Jack sat a little straighter, a look of, "Who's trying to put who on?" crossing his face.

"I'm serious, Jack. They were demons. And they were impersonating your dead ancestors."

"You don't think I'd fall for something like that, do you? Guardians, demons; they're all the same. There's no such thing."

"Demons are the angels or spirits that rebelled with Satan against God. They serve Satan. Their job is to gain control over humans and use them for the benefit of Satan."

"Come on, will you? This is the nuttiest thing you've ever tried to sell me. I mean, I can buy some of that God-stuff you've preached, but demons? Satan? Come on!"

Betsy said later that she really felt sympathetic to Jack. Only a short time before, as a *Christian,* she would have rejected most of what she was saying as being overly emotional or superstitious. But she had to tell him the truth.

"You see, when Bob allowed your Aunt Grace to hypnotize him when he was little, he opened himself up to evil powers. And the 'guardians' he saw and heard actually existed. The Bible says a lot about such things."

Jack began perspiring. Betsy thought it was the hot coffee and ignored it.

"And last night," she went on, "with the Lord's help, we cast all those demons out of Bob. He's free of them."

Jesse added, "That's why he's so happy this morning. He finally knows the real power of the Lord."

"Cast out? Wow, that must have been *some party* you all went to! Come on, Jesse. Let's go out and see what's happening around town. You need some fresh air."

"It's true, Jack," Jesse persevered. "Everything Betsy said. It was some party, all right, but the only spirits there were on their way out!"

Jack looked from Jesse to Betsy, and back. He was obviously agitated. "Who wouldn't be?" Betsy thought. "I don't know how I'd handle something like this about my own brother." Then she went on, "Jack, Bob has finally discovered what the power of Jesus Christ is all about. And you can, too. Wouldn't you like to have the same happiness that your brother has?"

"Are you kidding? You think I want to be like you freaks, with your spirits and stuff? I don't want to believe in the Lord. I want to live my life just like it is. I want to have fun."

"But look at the way things are," Jesse urged. "I mean, you can't say you're *happy* where you are. I know. I lived with you a while, remember? And look at your brother today. He's *really* happy. He's really having fun."

"I've got too many places to go and things to do. Don't try to hook me into your religious bit."

"But if you only knew the kind of powers that are around, wanting to get . . ."

Jack stood, verging on anger. "Look, lady, don't try to spook me with your evil spirits! The boogeyman is for kids!"

Both Betsy and Jesse saw that they were getting nowhere. If anything, they were further away. They must have both breathed a prayer at the same time — that same: "Lord, we're helpless again."

Then on an impulse, Jesse reached inside his shirt and pulled out the little wooden cross he had tied around his neck on a leather string. He slipped the string over his head and held it out toward Jack. "We won't push you, Jack. But why don't you take this and . . ." His sentence was never finished.

"Put that away!" Jack snapped, and jumped back a little.

Jesse was confused. He looked at his cross, wondering if there was something wrong with it. It looked as it always did, and he held it out again. "It's for you, Jack. It'll help you think about . . ."

"I said get it out of here!" Jack shouted, and he walked quickly into the living room.

Betsy and Jesse followed. "Is something wrong, Jack?" Betsy asked, as confused as Jesse by this sudden change.

"Nothing. It was just hot in there. I — I'm not feeling too good." That he was too warm and extremely uncomfortable was obvious. He ran an already-wet sleeve across his forehead. Jesse was trying to understand Jack's reaction. "It looked like you were afraid of this cross, Jack."

"Don't be nuts," Jack answered quickly. But all the time he was moving away from the cross in Jesse's outstretched hand. "Just put it away, will you?"

"I think *you're* the one who's nuts, Jack," Jesse commented as he kept moving toward him. "I know you don't want to accept the Lord, but to be afraid of a little hunk of wood is. . . ."

Jack's condition and attitude were very much like Bob's the night before when he had been sure "Aunt Grace" was approaching. And Betsy began to feel some of the same deep reactions to evil that we had all experienced. "Jesse . . ." she began, and stopped as she noticed Jesse was playing a strange game with Jack.

Using the cross as a kind of goad, Jesse was maneuvering Jack around the room. Jack was attempting to make his retreat seem like nervous pacing, but he never took his eyes off the object in Jesse's hand. "I really mean it, Jesse. Don't touch me with that thing."

"You have some sort of allergy to wood or leather?" Jesse prodded. "What are you afraid of?"

"Just forget it. Put it away. I mean it!"

"Are you afraid of the cross, Jack, or what it symbolizes?"

asked Betsy, trying to zero in on what she was sensing in his strange behavior. "You know that Jesus Christ was crucified on the cross. He took the punishment for all our sins straight there. You know that, don't you, Jack?"

Jack moved away, back into the kitchen. Jesse followed slowly, still extending the cross, and Betsy followed them. "You *do* know that, don't you, Jack?" she asked again.

But the boy that waited for them in the kitchen was a different person. He stood calmly, resting an arm on the top of the refrigerator, a small smile playing at the edges of his mouth. The perspiration which spotted his face and shirt seemed totally out of place, like beads of water on wax. And when he spoke, it was like Jack's voice and yet unlike it.

"It's no use," he said, and shook his head. It was not a statement of despair; it was more a statement of fact. At the words, a familiar chill ran through Jesse and Betsy. Jesse dropped his cross on the floor, and scooped it up quickly.

"What — what do you mean?" Betsy probed, thinking she knew the answer.

"He's mine," Jack replied coolly. "I've had him all this time, and you're not going to get him."

"Why do you want Jack?" Betsy addressed the one who spoke from Jack's body, and referred to Jack in the third person.

"I've had him since he was six. Ever since he started first grade, he's been mine." Here Jack's face began to contort in anger. He continued through clenched teeth: "You'll never get him! I know the future, and I can tell you, you'll never have him!" Then his attitude changed again. He looked at Betsy, and the thin line of his mouth widened into a smile. "You've never talked with Satan before, have you, Betsy?"

Although nothing unusual was seen or heard, the atmosphere seemed to quiver with energy. Satan! Betsy's mind screamed it. Could this conflict be so important as to summon the devil himself? Why did this have to happen when Tim wasn't home! "Lord, help!" her mind cried. But outwardly she remained as calm as possible.

"No," she said simply. "I haven't."*

Jack's expression looked almost wistful as he moved from the refrigerator and sat down casually on a kitchen chair. The perspiration stayed, seeming suspended, as though waiting for Jack's return and his need to register agitation.

"I could tell you *so* many things," he said, smiling at them in a way which was more disarming than they could have imagined possible. "You should have seen it when God and I were together. It was beautiful then. I was his greatest creation! His favorite! And he bestowed on me great power! And I do mean *great* power! But I wanted more. More!

"He told me about his creating this world and that he was going to bring many sons to himself. I wanted a world! I wanted to bring many sons to me! But he said, 'No! There is only one God.'

"I wanted to be great, as great as he was! Even greater! But he wouldn't let me. And I got angry.

"He made me leave. And I came *here.*"

At this point Jack sighed and blinked, as though the story had carried him away. Then, looking at Betsy and Jesse, he smiled and said, "You know, it's been a long time since I talked to anyone like this."

In the pause that followed, no one knew quite what to say. Was this an extremely clever charade by Jack? After the previous night, it might not be hard for demons to fool us into believing they were where they weren't. The thought passed through Betsy's mind: "What if Jack laughs and says something like, 'How's that for a demon? You're all too gullible!' "

Jesse spoke up. "Why don't you ask God to forgive you, and ask Jesus into your heart?"

"That's for *humans,* stupid! There is no forgiveness for me! I have no heart. Not in the sense you mean it! I am

---

*Though Tim and Betsy thought the evil spirit was Satan himself, they subsequently concluded it probably was not. Satan and demons are notorious deceivers, and Scripture recounts only rare confrontations between Satan and humans, such as the crucial encounters with Eve, Job, and Jesus. J.G.

what *I am!*" And then, as though suddenly remembering why he was there, he added, "and I'm going to keep Jack! You're not getting him. He's mine! I've got him. And I've got his *family!*"

Suddenly, in one sentence, there was the missing piece of the puzzle! Of course Satan had the whole family. Their home was an annex of hell. Jesse had called it a madhouse, and he was right. The idea of an entire family under the control of the devil was staggering.

But this revelation didn't have much time to settle. The telling of it started Jack's possesser bragging about his exploits. "Astonishing, isn't it — what I've been able to do with that family. The Lord hasn't a chance there!"

Betsy was about to mention Bob's experience but Jack chattered on before she could form the words.

"Remember the fire, the one that nearly destroyed their house? *I* started that. Or should I say I had *Jack* start it? He was getting too interested in what you were telling him about the Lord, and I couldn't allow that, could I?"

The fire had been a mystery until today. It had started in the garage, and it was one of those setbacks we came to expect in the early days of working with the brothers.

"I got him angry, see? So angry he kicked over a can of gasoline in the garage, and it burst into flames. It could have been a beautiful end to everything the Trammels have, but I wasn't able to delay the firetrucks." There was a note of bitterness in the admission, and Betsy and Jesse were again reminded that this evil power was not supreme.

"You're going to hell where you belong!" Jesse shouted.

"Yes," Jack's inhabitant admitted, "that's right. I am. But I'm taking Jack and a whole lot of others with me!"

"No, you're not," Betsy shouted. "God loves him, and Christ died for him, and he's going to *know* that! And," she added quietly but with firmness, "he's going to accept that!"

Jack's attitude changed again. He looked jovial, as though the scene was amusing. But the perspiration waited for its cue. "Look," he said affably, like a car salesman before his ridiculously low offer, "what do *you* want with him? Hasn't he been nothing but trouble to you? I can *use* him. I've got *plans* for him. Just leave him to me, and I'll take him off your hands. No more bother. He won't trouble you again. And neither will I. How about it?"

"It isn't that *we* want him," Betsy showed a flash of Spirit-directed insight. *"God* wants him. And we're going to help him."

"I've had him all these years," Jack's occupant continued. "I've spent a long time getting him ready." Then he turned to Jesse. "Jesse, you'll let me have him, won't you? I can make it worth your while. I really can. You know those Superman comics you used to like so much?"

Jesse looked startled at Jack's knowledge of his past. His answer was guarded. "Yeah?"

"Well, I can make you just like Superman. I mean it. Wouldn't you like to be the strongest man in the world? Able to leap tall buildings, and all that?"

"This is crazy!" Jesse looked at Betsy to see if he was hearing right. "Superman? This is just nuts!"

But Jack's expression was calm. "You don't believe that I have that kind of power? Try me. Leave Jack to me, join me against those who live dull, normal lives, and I'll give you powers that will thrill you all your life! Come on, Jesse. Give it a try."

The bizarre promise slipped comfortably into the events of the last few days. Even Betsy felt the lure of such power. She understood the hesitation in Jesse's attitude. "Lord, help," her mind cried again.

"Superman, huh?"

"Yes. Only not the comic book hero in a long red and blue suit; the real thing! Power! What's Jack to you when you compare him to what I'm offering? Come on, Jesse. Just try it out."

"O Lord," Betsy cried inside, "please free Jack! The devil's almost getting to Jesse. I'm no match for all this! Please! Help!"

"What are you guys doing?" broke in Jack — the real one. He stood up, looking genuinely puzzled. "What's going on?"

5

Round Two, Round Three, Round . . .

Jack looked at the kitchen clock. "Man, how did it get so late? I gotta get going. What are you starin' at me like that for?" He wiped the beaded perspiration from his forehead with his sleeve.

"Uhh, Jack," Betsy began dubiously. "Jack, don't you know what's been going on the last little while?"

"What do you mean, 'going on'?"

"Don't you know what you've been doing?" Jesse almost shouted.

"Sure. I've been trying to get you to put away that little charm of yours. And you did. So what?"

"But the *time,* Jack," Betsy again called his attention to the clock. "The time. Where did it all go?"

"You guys are kooky. How do I know what happened to

the time? I wasn't paying attention. Now, I really gotta go."

"Wait a minute." Betsy grabbed his arm with a strength that even surprised Jack. He pulled his arm away, and rubbed it involuntarily.

"Okay. What?"

"Jack, you've been in a kind of trance. The devil has been speaking out of you. At least he says he's the devil."

It was Jack's turn to stare. Then he broke into a smile. "Come on, will ya?"

"Jack, you just don't know how badly you need the Lord," Betsy continued. "Satan has *got* you, and if you don't get help from Jesus Christ you're going to end up with the devil forever."

Jack looked from Betsy to Jesse. They were both serious. No put-on. They were agreed that something very big was the matter. He started to say something, something that had none of the usual self-confidence in it. But his first word was cut off and his expression flashed to the unnatural calmness they had seen just a few minutes before.

"Look, let me tell you *my* side of the story," a now-familiar voice said from Jack. "Let me tell you what *really* happened. There's a lot you don't know."

This time Jesse and Betsy were not startled. It was almost as though they were talking to a fourth person in the kitchen, someone they didn't like but not someone who frightened them. "We don't want to hear it," Betsy said firmly.

"Nobody *ever* wants to listen to my side of it," Jack's inhabitor complained. "You're all narrow-minded! You only read what the Bible says about it. Wouldn't you like to know what really happened? I could tell you anything you wanted to know. How about it, Betsy? Any mystery of God or the universe — I could reveal to you. Go ahead, ask me whatever you want. You *know* I have the *power*. Try me on the *knowledge*."

It was tempting. A conversation with one who knew the world before this one was a fascinating prospect. Betsy began considering what she might ask — not really approving of such a conversation but savoring the thrill of a trial question.

And then it hit her: she was Eve all over again. Here was the devil offering her wisdom, offering a look into things beyond human experience. And she was beginning to succumb! She could feel a sensation of evil power touching her.

Suddenly she was praying out loud. She shouted her prayer in order to block the sound of the tempter's penetrating voice getting through. "In the name of Jesus Christ I command you to leave!"

But Jack kept on talking, kept on offering a look into the mysteries of past ages. Betsy panicked. The words kept coming and the face kept smiling, like a face on the television screen that continues talking, with no attention to its live, home audience.

"God is able," Betsy's mind insisted. "It is *his* power that is effective here, not mine. I have none. O, Lord, fill me with *your* power. Have your Holy Spirit handle this which is so far beyond me! Please."

And again her mind and her feeling were working together. She experienced a calmness, a deafness against what was coming from Jack's mouth. She knew that God was present, and again she shouted: "In the name and power of Jesus Christ, I command you to leave!"

And Jack was quiet.

There was little time to reflect, but a new thought leaped through Betsy's mind. She was seeing that faith was specific. She had known that God was able to overcome evil; she knew Bible verses which showed God to be the ultimate victor over the devil and all his works. But she had not had a simple faith which could say: "The Lord wants to stop this right now." But as she experienced his presence she was able to give the immediate situation to him.

"I . . . I don't get it," Jack was saying to Jesse. "I mean, what you're saying is nuts."

"But that's what's happening to you, Jack. It really *is*. We start talking to you about the Lord and all of a sudden you're a different guy. And this voice comes out of you, and . . ."

"Why don't you let him alone?" rasped the voice again.

In her weariness Betsy wanted to say, "Why don't *you* leave *us* alone?" If only there would be time to gather strength or talk about the next move.

"I need Jack. I've got big plans for him. He can help me at school. And he's going to help me later when he goes into the Navy. I've got big plans. Leave him alone!"

"God has big plans for him," Jesse blurted. "He has big plans for every one of us." And then, almost playfully, he tossed a barb at Jack's speaker. "He even has some pretty big plans for you, doesn't he?"

There was a short pause in which both Betsy and Jesse relished their direct hit. And then a grimace began spreading across Jack's face that destroyed their enjoyment. It was pure rage — a twisted fury. It seemed completely foreign to the face that was forming it. They were frightened.

"Do you think yourselves wise to defy me? Do you really think you are protected against what I could do with a snap of Jack's finger? You are able to talk with me only because *I allow it!* I could turn you into raving lunatics as easily as . . ."

"No, you couldn't!" Betsy retorted. "Jesus Christ is almighty! And we are his and he is ours!"

The distorted face didn't change — it stared. And it spoke quietly. "If you are so secure in your faith, my dear Betsy, why are you shouting? Do you really think that you have the faith to pull this off? You who can't even trust your God for money for a new car? Do you think faith like that has any effect against me?"

Again the psychological slant of the confrontation had shifted. Both Betsy and Jesse began praying again. The enemy's low-keyed but relentless challenge had moved them to the defensive.

"You're going to end up the loser!" Jesse threatened. Though it was true, it was a feeble effort, and they all knew it.

Jack didn't move. Only his eyes shifted to Jesse. Betsy had a fleeting thought: "If only they'd blink!" But before another word was said the telephone rang. Another thought popped in Betsy's mind: "If only that was an alarm clock and I'd wake up!"

"H-hello." Betsy's voice was shaking. Somehow it had remained strong in the conversation, but in this brief moment of relief it began to fall apart.

"Betsy?"

"Yes."

"I didn't recognize you. Have you got a cold?"

"No." Betsy recognized her friend, Ruth. "I-I'm just in the middle of something. Can I call you back?"

"Sure thing. It can wait. Are you sure you're all right?"

"Yes, Ruth. Fine. Really."

"I just wanted to tell you a few things I've been reading about demons and all that. I looked up all those verses you told me about, and maybe there really *is* something to it all."

"Yeah. Maybe." Betsy bit at a fingernail.

Ruth went on. "One thing seems pretty sure, Betsy. When Jesus was face-to-face with the devil, he started quoting Scripture. That's how he battled him. You sure couldn't fight like that on your own, in your own strength or faith. You really need Scripture. It's God's fight."

Betsy let out a short, chopped laugh. "Thank you, Ruth."

"Huh? What for? Are you sure you're . . ."

"Thank you for calling and telling me what God wanted me to know. I'll talk to you later. 'Bye."

Betsy replaced the receiver before Ruth had finished a puzzled "Goodbye," and started back into the living room with a grateful smile.

But she wasn't ready for the sight that awaited her. Jack was bent over Jesse, shouting, and his hands were clamped around Jesse's throat. Jesse's face was red and his eyes were bulging. Betsy ran to the struggling boys and began pounding on Jack's back but it was futile.

Betsy stumbled back. Jesse was gasping for air. She knew there was nothing she could do physically. And then Ruth's words about faith and strength and Scripture flooded her mind.

"Use *your* power, Lord. Only yours! We are powerless

against this enemy!" The anguish in her prayer had closed her eyes. And when she opened them again, she saw both Jesse and Jack sitting dazed on the floor. Jesse was rubbing his throat. Jack was looking around, obviously confused as to how he got where he was. "O Lord, thank you," Betsy sighed.

"What in the world . . ." Jack muttered, brushing his hair out of his eyes and standing. "What's going on?" He began trying to brush the wrinkles out of his shirt.

"You just tried to kill me," Jesse answered grimly, standing and still rubbing his throat.

"You're nuts," Jack said, but his tone was less confident than the words. "I wouldn't do that to you."

"What does this look like?" Jesse said, raising his chin to show Jack the red and white lines which marked his throat.

"That's crazy," Jack said. "It's just crazy. I wouldn't do that."

"Maybe not," Betsy entered the conversation. "But *he* would."

"You gonna go back to that devil stuff again? Well, forget it! He wouldn't do that to me, neither!"

Probably the excitement blurred Jack's reference to double personalities, but later Betsy and Jesse would recall it as a breakthrough.

"Yes, he would," Jesse declared. "Look, man, I know. I got the burning skin to prove it. Where were you? How did you get all messed up? Why don't you know what you just did?"

Jack was obviously puzzled, but he was unwilling to admit anything had conquered him. The confrontation seemed stalemated. In a kind of desperation move, Betsy excused herself and telephoned me. She said things were out of hand, and she didn't get very far into describing the events before I said I'd be right home.

Returning, Betsy found the living room and then the kitchen deserted. There was a moment of panic. Had Jack and Jesse left while she was on the phone? Were they still in the house somewhere? The silence was ominous.

Then sounds of struggle from the utility room reached

her ears. Quickly she ran to the partially opened door — Jack and Jesse were again locked in combat. They appeared to be a tableau, a statue, frozen at the point of kill. Jack had a sharp kitchen knife against Jesse's chest, and Jesse was exerting every ounce of strength to keep its point from entering him.

For a moment Betsy was frozen too. Then she made a grab for the knife and was amazed as it slid easily out of Jack's hand. No struggle. It was like lifting a knife from the hands of a statue.

And almost immediately Jack was again in control of himself. And again he was confused as to how he got into such a position.

"I've got to get home," Jack said anxiously. He repeated it a number of times but made no move toward the door. Betsy was determined to keep him there until I could arrive and see for myself what was going on, and strangely, like the seizing of the knife, there seemed no trouble in detaining Jack.

"You look hungry," Betsy said. It was a wild play, but Jack had always seemed interested in food.

"Yeah," he agreed.

"Let me fix the two of you some sandwiches. It's after one o'clock."

"One?" Jack jumped to his feet. Then, realizing his surprise was an admission of guilt, he sat back down, trying to hide the confusion on his face.

Jesse wasn't about to miss the opening. "That's right, Jack. After one. You came here about ten-thirty or eleven, right?"

"So what if I did?" Jack was admitting nothing, but it was obvious his mind was racing for explanations.

"Well, where'd the time go?"

Betsy was making cheese sandwiches. She shuddered as an old saying flashed through her mind: "How time flies when you're having fun."

Jack replied defensively, "I . . . I just wasn't paying attention. Get off, will you?"

Betsy began quoting Scripture. We had marked a few

passages at the youth conference. Now the Bible in the kitchen opened readily to those places.

"Then this wicked one will appear, whom the Lord Jesus will burn up with the breath of his mouth and destroy by his presence when he returns."

"Since we, God's children, are human beings — made of flesh and blood — he became flesh and blood, too, by being born in human form; for only as a human being could he die, and in dying break the power of the devil who had the power of death."

The sandwiches were ready, and Betsy brought them to the table. Jesse looked up at her with a mournful expression; a quick glance at Jack showed why. His expression was smug, much as a bully gloats over the struggle of a weakling.

"You won't let him hear the Scripture, will you!" Betsy charged.

"Huh? What do you mean?" Jack replied.

"Aw, come on, man," Jesse said disgustedly. "We know you're back."

"What are you talking about?" Jack asked again. Jesse wasn't in the frame of mind to play games. He flipped out the small cross that had started the whole thing and thrust it in front of Jack's face. "This!" he shouted.

Jack recoiled, lifting his arm in front of his eyes.

Jesse put the cross back in his pocket, and Jack lowered his arm. As he lowered it, his expression changed to admission of being caught and a cover-up amusement.

"Okay," Jack sighed. Then he concentrated on his sandwich, nibbling warily. "Aren't you going to call Tim, Betsy?"

"I already did," she said.

He glanced up. "I didn't see you do that. Hmmmm." He took another bite. "He's on the way home, eh?"

"That's right."

"He believe what you told him? About me?"

"He's coming home."

Jack took another disinterested bite. "I almost had both

of you once, you know. Oh, not together. I almost had you about two years ago. Remember?"

That moment almost undermined what little courage Betsy had been able to muster. Of course she remembered. Two years ago she had gone through a terrible depression, complete with sleepless nights and loss of nearly all the faith she had. She was questioning the existence of God and making herself and everyone around her miserable.

"But, look," broke in Jack. "You and Tim are in the hands of your Lord. Okay. But why take my Jack? I need him. I've only got three years left."

Jesse sat up. "Three years? You mean, before Jesus comes back?"

"That's right," Jack went on. "Only three years."

Jesse didn't say it, but his mouth formed a "Wow!" He looked as though he had been handed the secret of the ages and the weight of knowing when history would run out was almost too much.

"Wait a minute," Betsy protested. "The Bible says that no one but God himself knows what time that will be. You're putting us on again."

Jack smiled that amused "caught me" smile. "Not bad, but I hooked ol' Jesse, here!" And he laughed.

Betsy began to wonder what was keeping me. With this antagonist playing games, replacements were necessary. "I'm going to check and see if Tim's coming," she finally said, half-aloud.

"Don't worry," her visitor said. "I haven't done anything to him." But the way he said it threw Betsy into a shaky state. She all but ran to the phone to call my office.

6

Countdown

"He left right after you called," my associate told Betsy. "Should be there anytime now."

"Thanks, Bernie," Betsy said, replacing the phone with a feeling of dread. Normally it takes me from fifteen minutes to half an hour to get home, depending on traffic, and that fifteen-minute difference isn't noticed. But today every minute more than the minimum hinted to Betsy I might be in a ditch or who-knows-where.

Betsy walked back into the kitchen. She had begun to tense up before re-entering the "battle field," and she wasn't prepared for the serenity that met her. Jesse and Jack were sitting at the table in quiet conversation. But her immediate relief was instantly dissipated as she took a seat beside the boys.

"Nothing to it," Jack was saying. "I can make you anything you want to be. None of this waiting for something in the sweet bye-and-bye that may or may not happen. I'm talking about right now, Jesse. You name it. You come to me, and it's yours."

Betsy gasped, but the sound didn't seem to register on either Jesse's or Jack's ears. They were only hearing each other and the "wall" around them was thick.

"Oh, no, Lord," Betsy prayed. "He's such a young Christian. Please, Lord. Don't let him fall. Please, Lord. It's your power. I know I can't do a thing. Please, dear God, by your Spirit protect Jesse right now."

And Jesse began to laugh. The laugh caught Jack by surprise. "What's so funny? Don't you believe me?"

"Sure, I believe you *can* do it. But the Lord gives me everything I need right now. He gives me love like you know nothing about. And he gives me peace — I've seen the kind of 'peace' you give. And he gives me eternal life. Man, you can't touch any of that." And Jesse laughed again.

Betsy laughed, too, in enormous relief. And as if to punctuate their laughter, the sound of my car coming in the driveway seemed to put things on a more even keel.

It had been all I could do to drive within the speed limit. My mind was afire with the few things Betsy had hurriedly told me on the phone, and I wanted to floor the accelerator. But the Lord seeemed to be saying to me, "Wouldn't Satan like to tie you up with a policeman? Drive carefully. You'll get there faster." Almost immediately after this impression I saw a police car sitting off to the side of the street, just waiting for me had I been in too much of a hurry. God is practical.

But there was no fine for running between the car and the back door, and I ran. I thought I was ready for almost anything as I pushed the door open in to the kitchen, but I didn't expect to see Betsy and Jesse laughing. As I entered, Jack turned around, and he was smiling, too. I was off balance.

"What are you doing home?" Jack asked cheerfully.

What could I say? The scene was cheerful and the

familiar setting reassuring. Betsy's urgent summons and my churning thoughts seemed unreal. Unless . . . my mind flashed to an old science-fiction movie on television where cosmic invaders hid in people's bodies and the Dr. Jekyl-Mr. Hyde conflict was not discovered until it was too late for the earthlings. Could all three be . . . ?

"O Tim, I'm so glad to see you," Betsy said, running to me and holding on. The tears in her eyes showed me she had been through almost more than she could bear.

"Yeah, man, we really need help," Jesse added, and the situation began to come clear.

"Is he still . . . ?" I half-whispered to Betsy, and she nodded that he was still in the power of his evil companion.

I stepped closer to the table, studying Jack's face. He looked down and took a small bite of the sandwich in his hand. He looked normal, I thought. He was obviously aware I was studying him, and he seemed to be enjoying it. Jack, I thought, would have probably been angered at my staring. Finally, I said, "Demon, I've come to claim Jack for the Lord. You've got no right to him. God loves him and Christ shed his blood for him."

"That's true enough," the voice like Jack's said, without looking up from the sandwich. "But *he's* got to make the choice. And he'll never do it. I *know* the future. Jack will never go with the Lord." There was no anger, no shouting. He said it flatly and simply.

I had to talk to Jack: "In the name and power of Jesus Christ and his shed blood, I command you to leave!" And Jack was free again.

He took a hungry bite from the sandwich in his hand. "Ummm, this is good," he said, looking up. When he saw me, he jumped a little, and then smiled.

"Hi, Tim. Didn't see you come in. You home from work already? Hey, will you set these people right? You should hear the crazy stuff they're telling me. All about the devil being in me, and all that. It's nuts. I mean it."

I knew this wasn't the time to beat around the bush. We were never sure how long we had with Jack before he'd be taken over again, and every second with him was important. "It's not Jesse or Betsy who need straightening out, Jack. It's you," I began.

Jack's eyes rolled upward in an expression of: "Here we go again." He stood up. "Look, I've had all the scary talk I need for one day. I'm gonna split. You three just sit around and have your little séances if you want to. I've got better things to do."

"Jack," I said with more force than I'd expected. "Sit back down. This is more important to you than anything else you'll ever have to go through." And to my surprise, he sat.

"There's a battle going on right now, Jack, and you're right in the middle of it. And you'd better face up to it. It's real. And it's *for you;* I mean, for your eternal soul. Listen to me, Jack. Satan's got you. I don't know how or why he's got so much power over you, but he has, and he's not about to give up without a struggle. He keeps you from hearing the Bible. He keeps you from hearing the kind of things I'm telling you right now . . ."

"And he keeps Jack from paying any attention to any of you!" The voice coming out of Jack was shocking in its stridency. Jack was gone again.

"Lord," I prayed out loud, "how can we get through to Jack if you allow Satan back every time? Please, Lord, cast him out!"

"Cast him out?" Jack's speaker was almost incensed. "You don't cast Satan out. You *bind* him!"

I didn't understand why he would help me like that! The devil must have supreme ego to be bothered by wrong terminology about him. I prayed for his power to be bound, in the power of the blood of Jesus Christ. Jack was back, and I felt we didn't have much time.

"Betsy, Jesse," I said hastily, "Pray! You pray! I'll talk. Maybe among the three of us . . ."

Jack was dazed. "What's all the excitement? What's been going on?"

"Listen carefully, Jack," I started again. "There's a real battle going on for your soul right now. And it won't be settled until *you* decide who will win. It's up to you, Jack. If you choose to ask forgiveness and trust Jesus Christ, you'll have the power of his Spirit living in you. Jesus said, 'I am the way, the truth, and the life. No one can get to the Father except by means of me.' "

Jack was still with us. Betsy and Jesse were praying with all the intensity they possessed. And words almost flew from my mouth.

"Satan is just the opposite, Jack. He only wants to destroy you! That's all. And you can't fight him without Jesus Christ. But we can't do any more than tell you about him, Jack. The decision has to be yours! You have to accept Jesus Christ, and join the winning force against the devil, or simply stay where you are, spiritually, and go to hell with him. It's your life, Jack! And it's your death."

I stopped and waited. Jack was trembling. Thank God he had stayed with us the whole way without another visitation. He just sat, shaking.

"How about it, Jack?" I pressed.

And then his shaking stopped. He seemed calm, then with a deadly smile he looked up and I saw he was no longer with us.

"Tim," he said in a friendly way, "that was okay. I mean, I admire your sincerity. But I've got him. Now, why don't you and I just go on out to Toby's and have one for old times' sake?"

I could hardly believe my ears.

The enemy was back, and more devilish, if that's possible, than ever. He hadn't been bound at all. Even his "theology" was a lie. I remembered, then, that it was Christ who bound Satan, not the believer. This had been another way of tying us up, making us ineffective, playing on our too-little knowledge of the Scripture.

I hadn't thought of Toby's in maybe ten years. It was a little bar where I could have been found almost every night for a period of about two years, drinking myself into oblivion. How would he know about Toby's?

"What do you say, Tim? Remember the good old days? Sure, we all got a little smashed at times, but it was great fun, wasn't it? You used to play 'Sentimental Me' on that old juke box that Toby never changed the records on, and . . ."

"Stop it!" I shouted. The whole thing was almost too much! He sounded like one of my old drinking buddies. It brought back too many feelings, too many memories. "That's not me anymore," I said, gaining composure. "That's the past. It's dead."

"Toby's is still there," the voice reported. "And so is that old juke box. And so are some of the old gang you . . ."

"That's not me anymore," I said forcefully. And inside I thanked God it wasn't. "I am new. That's all dead. My Bible says, 'When someone becomes a Christian he becomes a brand new person inside. He is not the same anymore. A new life has begun!' And I can tell you that's all dead! The past is dead history! Jesus Christ lives in me!"

When I finished I felt the way a preacher must feel who gets carried away in the preaching of his sermon. There was a brief pause, and I didn't quite know what to say next. And the enemy was strangely low in his response.

"Yes, I know. I know." Then he raised his tone. "All right, so I don't have you. Any of you. But let me have Jack. I need him, and he's of no use to you."

Betsy suddenly spoke up. "That's what he said before, Tim. But be careful. He gets you to thinking that you have the power to give or keep Jack. I didn't think of it until later."

She was right. "This is God's fight," I said.

"It may be," the voice said. "But you're on the wrong side. You're no match for me."

"What are you talking about?" I responded. I could feel a sense of power in me that was certainly from the Lord. "You've been beaten already. You were defeated at Calvary by the cross!"

Suddenly Jack laughed. It was enough to stop all praying. "The cross?" He laughed again. "You think I was beaten by *the cross?*"

Jesse sprang to his feet from the corner chair where he'd been sitting and produced his little wooden cross. "That's right!" he shouted triumphantly, and he thrust the little cross in front of Jack. "The cross!"

Jack's arm went up, shielding it from his view. But the voice which had been laughing took on that terrible shrillness it had a few minutes before. The sound was somewhere between a scream and a wail as it filled the room: "It wasn't the cross! It was the *blood!* The *blood!* The *blood!*"

The words seemed to echo through the house. We were all stunned by their force. Verses flashed through all our minds.

"Without the shedding of blood there is no forgiveness of sins."

"But if we are living in the light of God's presence, just as Christ does, then we have wonderful fellowship and joy with each other, and the blood of Jesus his Son cleanses us from every sin."

The cross that Jack couldn't look at was only a symbol, a reminder.

"He took this list of sins and destroyed it by nailing it to Christ's cross. In this way God took away Satan's power to accuse you of sin, and God openly displayed to the whole world Christ's triumph at the cross where your sins were all taken away."

As the words, "The blood" began to fade from our minds, we found ourselves murmuring, "Jesus, Jesus, Jesus . . ." As if in response, Jack's eyes blinked and he was back with us.

"Was he back?" Jack asked. It was a surprising question from the boy who wouldn't admit the influence of an invisible being.

"Yes."

"What did he say?"

"He wants you for himself, Jack. He won't give up without a struggle." Betsy and Jesse were praying again, spurred on by this small shift in Jack's attitude, and the possible return of the adversary. "You know he has you, don't you, Jack?" I asked.

· And after a long pause, Jack said simply, "Yes, since I was fourteen."

Betsy drew a quick breath, but returned to praying immediately. Jesse wanted to say something, but followed Betsy's example.

"He told me a lot of things and promised me a lot," Jack continued quietly. "He showed me a lot of what he can do."

"But don't you see, Jack," I implored as I tried to push aside the thousand distracting questions which flooded my mind, "all he wants to do is destroy you. That's all he wants to do with anyone. He wants to take you and as many as he can with him when he lands in hell. And then, Jack, it's just too late to change your mind."

"But I know so many things you can't even think of."

"And what good will they do you in hell?"

"Wouldn't you like to know just a few of the things that I do? There's all kinds of power you could . . ."

"Jack, I can't let you talk like this, if it really is you talking. Sure, I'm curious. But no information, true or false, is worth giving up my soul for. You're more valuable than that, Jack. Jesus died for you."

Then, like a splice in a film, Jack changed again. His voice and actions were sharp and staccatto. "I've had enough! All right, so you got him to tell you a little. That's all! He's mine. And if you don't leave him alone, I will kill him!"

We all froze at the thought, and Jack's visitor went on, "Never mind chasing me away. I'm going. But if you don't leave him alone by eight o'clock tonight, I'll take him. And if you think I'm playing games, just try me! Eight o'clock tonight! That's it!"

"He was here again," Jack mumbled.

"That's right."

"What'd he say this time?"

"I . . . I don't know how to tell you. He said if we didn't leave you to him — leave you alone — by eight o'clock tonight, he'd . . . he'd take you with him."

"Kill me?"

"Yeah."

There was a long silence. Jesse and Betsy had stopped

praying. The invader had said he would stay away until eight. None of us knew what to say or do. One by one, we drifted into the living room and sat down. We were tired and depressed. We were at a loss.

I had to go on with Jack, but it was a struggle to get started. "Don't you see the mess you're in, Jack? He may have promised you the world, but when things get hot, he's going to kill you rather than let you get away. Don't you see how desperately you need the Lord? You've got to ask Jesus Christ to come into your heart and life before it's too late."

"I . . . I can't."

"But why can't you? What's holding you back?"

"I don't know. I just can't."

"I'm going to read some Scripture to you, Jack, and I pray the Lord will keep you with us to hear it."

"And what is it that God has said? That he has given us eternal life, and that this life is in his Son. So whoever has God's Son has life; whoever does not have his Son, does not have life."

I looked up from the Bible. It was hard to tell, but it looked as though Jack was still listening as Jack.

"Those who let themselves be controlled by their lower natures live only to please themselves, but those who follow after the Holy Spirit find themselves doing those things that please God. Following after the Holy Spirit leads to life and peace, but following after the old nature leads to death, because the old sinful nature within us is against God. It never did obey God's laws and it never will."

I looked up again. Jack's clothes were soaking with perspiration, but he was listening. "That's what I'm offering you, Jack. Imagine! A life that will *please God!* After everything you've done, imagine the love of God who would forgive you and remake you into a child of his, doing things which will please him. Jack, this is serious business. This is salvation or destruction. This is heaven or hell. Nobody's fooling around this time."

"Only two more hours!" the voice from Jack shrieked.

Then Jack was with us again. "What did it say?"

"He's getting angry. He says, 'Only two more hours.' "

"Oh, man . . ." Jack was in agony. "Two hours, huh?"

He looked like a trapped animal. And we shared some of his trapped feelings.

"Can he really do that?" Betsy asked me quietly. "I mean can he just . . . just kill Jack like that?"

"I don't know," I confessed. But immediately I corrected myself. "No, he can't. God sets the limits." But what God's specific will was for Jack I didn't know.

"Maybe we should place a call to the Gibsons," Betsy ventured. "They seemed to have been through most of this before."

"Good idea," I said, standing. Before going to the phone, I looked around the room. Jack was huddled in the corner of the sofa, looking half-whipped and half-frightened. I was struck with the similarity of his pose to his brother's the night before in the car; reminiscent of pictures I'd seen of mental patients. Jesse was sitting on the floor, his back against the coffee table, looking as dejected as I'd ever seen anyone. Betsy sat sideways in a chair, looking at me with the pain of helplessness.

Then it struck me. "Wait a minute, gang," I said, almost too loudly for the circumstances. "Jack isn't dead yet. Why are we holding the funeral now? Is our God the God of power and control, or isn't he? I'm going to make this phone call, and then I think we'd better see about this giving in to the death thing before anything has really happened."

There was a general stirring and changing of positions. Little flickers of hope flashed here and there. But only briefly. Jack suddenly shouted in an all-too-familiar voice, "Eight o'clock! And that's it!" And he was back to himself immediately.

"Wow, Tim, I don't know what to tell you," Bill Gibson said after I'd pretty well laid out what we'd been through. "Sounds like you're into something a lot more complex than we've experienced."

"What about this death threat, Bill? Can he do it?"

"I just don't know, Tim. Wait a minute. Here's what I

was looking for. In Revelation, right up front, where Jesus says to John, 'Don't be afraid! Though I am the First and Last, the Living One who died, who is now alive forevermore, who has the keys of hell and death — don't be afraid!' "

"That's pretty powerful."

"I'll say. And he says right there that he has the keys of hell and death. In other words, the devil *can't* kill Jack unless the Lord permits it. And from what you've told me about the two times he tried to kill Jesse, I'd say the power of life and death is *not* there."

I reported back to the living room what the conversation brought out, and suggested that this was just a scare tactic. But the occasional breaking in of that devilish voice, reminding us of the threat and the time, made faith difficult.

We spent most of the two hours praying and reading the Scriptures. Jack listened, we hoped. It was hard to tell what was going on in him. Most of the time he sat staring, frightened, without a move or response.

After a while I began to feel that we were kind of selfish. Betsy, Jesse and I were reading the Bible and praying while Jack was touching hell. What we should be doing was cheering him up; getting his mind off his coming confrontation. We should all drive down to the root beer stand and talk about something light, something diverting.

But as I began to form the suggestion in words, I realized this line of thinking was yet another distraction. "Lord, forgive me," I prayed inside, "and show us what we should do. Time is running out!"

It was so obvious. I hardly had the prayer expressed before the Lord indicated: "Jack needs to accept my gift of salvation." We had gotten so distracted, looking up verses about the devil's power and guessing at his ability to do this and that. We were trying to comfort *ourselves* in this crazy situation. My feelings that we were being selfish were right, but we were being subtly guided away from the real issue: Jack's salvation.

"Jack, there isn't a whole lot of time left, and you still haven't accepted the only way out. Jack . . ."

"He's coming again, Tim," Jack blurted out. "I can feel him coming back again! He's got me!"

"Pray, Jack," I pleaded. But it was too late. His eyes flashed as he shouted, "Leave him alone! Or I will take him! I'll take him in two minutes!"

"But you said eight o'clock!"

"Two minutes!"

And again Jack slumped back into the sofa. "What . . . what did he say?"

"He said two minutes."

"Two minutes? Did he really say that? Are you sure?"

"Two minutes."

"But he told me I was really going to be great. He told me . . ."

"When, Jack? When did he tell you all this?"

"A long time ago. The other day. I don't remember. He was going to show me how to go places without using cars or airplanes. He was going to show me how to talk to great people who were already dead. He was . . ."

"Jack, listen!" I was shouting now, because I was very conscious of the second hand ticking its way around my watch. "All that stuff, even if you *could* do it, wouldn't matter. You'd end up with Satan right smack in the middle of hell! Jesus wants to free you from the devil's power. He can free you, and live in you, and make *you*, Jack, pleasing to God. Saved from the torture of being the devil's puppet here, and free from eternal damnation. I'm giving it to you straight, Jack, because there's . . ."

"One minute!" the voice coming from Jack finished my sentence. Then Jack spoke again. "What'd he say?"

"One minute."

Jack's face was running perspiration.

"What's holding you back, Jack? It isn't difficult. All you have to do is ask Jesus to come into your life. And mean it! You don't have to change first. He will change you. But you have to give him the invitation. *You* have to open the door!"

"I . . . I want to. But I . . . can't. Something keeps telling me, 'No!' "

"Don't you know who that is? Come on, Jack!"

"Thirty seconds!" Jack's enemy announced wildly.

"How much time?" Jack asked.

"Thirty seconds," I answered almost frantically. "I'm watching the clock."

"Are you sure it's only thirty seconds?"

"That's what he said, Jack. It's up to you now. Do you want the Lord in your life, or do you want this monster to rule it? Now, Jack!"

"I . . . I want the Lord."

"Well, then, let's pray!"

And with about ten seconds left, Jack and I fell on our knees in the living room, and Jack said, "Lord Jesus, take me. Help me. I want you, and not him."

We all were about to breathe a sigh of exhausted relief when Jack's voice once again changed. "All right," he scowled. "He did it. The Lord's got his foot in the door. I have to go now. But not for long. I'll be back. I'll be back!" And Jack fell over onto the floor.

We lifted him onto the sofa, and shook him awake. He opened his eyes, almost afraid of what he might see, and then asked, "Is it all over?"

"Yes," I assured him. "How do you feel?"

His answer was weak but sincere: "Great. I feel just great."

7

"I Told You I'd Be Back"

In Luke 4:13 the Scripture says, "When the devil had ended all the temptations, he left Jesus for a while (the older version says 'for a season') and went away." I'd like to be able to write that the story of spiritual battle ends here after Jack's commitment. I'd like to write that the brothers lived without demon oppression after that, but it isn't true.

When Jack left our home the night of the great struggle, Betsy, Jesse, and I were exhausted. The two days spent with the brothers had been taxing beyond description, and we were ready to sleep the sleep of victory. But the enemy went away only "for a season."

As I was making notes on our experiences I remembered that Bob, when given the chance, had not actually asked Jesus in to fill the space left by his Guardians. Betsy and I had been drained of emotion and energy at the time and we rested. But the victory was not complete.

The morning following Jack's battle with the evil spirit, Bob pounded on our door. He was as radiant as we'd ever seen him, and we praised God all over again for his deliverance. Over coffee, we asked if he'd had a chance to talk with his brother about what had happened.

"Jack got in pretty late. I was too sleepy to talk so I pretended to be asleep. And I got out before he was awake this morning."

"Then you don't know."

"Know what?"

Betsy and I exchanged a smug glance. I said, "Well, last night Jack finally gave himself to the Lord."

Bob looked at me for a long moment and then turned to Betsy. Her bright nod in agreement convinced him we weren't fooling.

"Man, I can't understand that at all," he finally said, very troubled.

We had expected him to cheer with delight. This was a difficult reaction to handle. "What's the matter?"

"Well, when he came in about two this morning, he was . . ."

"Two?" Betsy cut in. "He left here about nine last night."

"Well, it was two when he got home and I know Jack — he was drunk."

Betsy moaned in distress. "It was such a long, hard fight — and he finally said *'yes'* to God. What could have happened?"

"I don't know," Bob said. "I didn't know anything about it."

Waves of fatigue washed back over us. We'd been through the whole thing with Bob and then with Jack, and now it seemed that it was wasted agony as far as Jack was concerned. Where was God's power in all this? Why didn't he move in and solidify what he had started?

"Maybe . . . maybe you could talk with him," I suggested lamely to Bob.

"No, sir." Bob was decisive, his hands raised in a "stop"

gesture. "I like my life the way it is. I don't want any more of that demon stuff. He can have it if he wants. I'm staying away from him."

That seemed to settle that. The brothers had been extremely close until now, probably because everyone else was afraid of them. Now they were divided. I remember thinking it was ironic that Bob should express a fear of his brother. His decision to stay away from Jack, however, was short-lived, for our back door opened and there was Jack.

"Hi, everybody," he said cheerfully.

To say we were a little tense is putting it mildly. We returned his "Hi," and Betsy asked if he'd like a cup of coffee. In a minute or two we were sitting around the kitchen table, looking a little like professional gamblers, trying to read expressions and gauge the strength of each others' cards.

"How are you this morning?" Betsy ventured after a period of uncomfortable silence.

"Great!" Jack came back, almost too fast. "Just great."

There was another pause as we all tried to find something to say. Then, surprisingly, Bob jumped in with both feet.

"Jack, you really have to get serious with the Lord. I mean it. You can't play it both ways."

A little tingle went through me to hear Bob's quiet sincerity. Only two days before he had been such a pathetic victim of evil and now he was tuned in to real freedom.

"I mean it, Jack. I know what it's like on both sides. And having Jesus is really where it's at."

"Wooo-wooo!" Jack suddenly made a sound like a freight train.

We all froze, thrown for a loss by this bizarre behavior.

"I'm serious, Jack," Bob said with an uncertain smile.

"Wooo-wooo! Beeep-beeep!" Jack responded. Then he took a mouthful of coffee and gargled loudly.

I can't remember a time in my life when I felt so disoriented. In the past few days I'd gotten used to struggling with demons, but to have a normal-appearing youth making infantile faces and noises like a train strained my reason!

Bob brought perspective to the lunacy of the scene.

"Poor Jack," he said softly. He leaned toward his brother. "I'm free, Jack. My Guardians are buried. I'm free. And you need to be, too."

Jack laughed. "Thirteen little guardians up on the shelf. One came out-a-the box, and then there were twelve. Twelve little guardians kicked out of heaven. One came out-a-the box and then there were eleven. Eleven guardians . . ."

We all got the message, and Bob suddenly drew back. "Are you sure those Guardians can't get back from where you sent them?" he asked me, white-faced.

Jesus' words in Matthew 12 raced into my mind. "For if the demon leaves, it goes into the deserts for a while, seeking rest but finding none. Then it says, 'I will return to the man I came from.' So it returns and finds the man's heart clean but empty! Then the demon finds seven other spirits more evil than itself, and all enter the man and live in him. And so he is worse off than before."

"I thought you said they were buried for good." Bob's eyes burned as his words stung me.

Jack laughed.

"Could they come back?" Bob shifted in his chair, then jumped up and began pacing. Fear had taken over, and his confidence in Christ was deteriorating visibly. I felt desperate. I didn't know whether his Guardians could or would come back.

Jack continued to laugh oddly, reminding me of the stuffed figures I'd seen in front of carnival fun houses. His happy expression never changed, but his eyes were mirthless and blank. His laugh seemed somehow recorded, not the same laugh as his mouth was forming. Betsy and I sensed that we were in for a terrible struggle.

"The Lord!" I shouted over Jack's laugh to the pacing youth. "He can keep you safe from them. It's *his* strength! *His* power! None of us are up to this kind of battle, but *he* is! Hang on to the Lord!"

Bob suddenly stopped moving about the kitchen as if a switch in him had been turned off.

"The Lord!" he spat contempuously. And Jack's laughing

stopped instantly. The room was terrifyingly silent. Betsy and I glanced from Bob to Jack: we were confronted by evil ones in both brothers at once.

The stream of profanity and blasphemy that belched from Bob's mouth still haunts me. I have often wished that my hearing had been jammed during that outbreak. There are times, even today, when the words and phrases scream in my mind, and only prayer shuts them up. The devil is more sordid than any of us realize, and one vile eruption of his anger against God can deeply stain the soul.

Betsy clamped her hands over her ears and ran from the room, praying. I sank to my knees in the kitchen, pleading with God to release Bob and Jack. Soon I sensed a change in the room and looked up. Jack seemed to be dazed, but himself. He was staring at Bob who was also on his knees, his face contorted, his speech diabolical.

"Help me now, O Satan! Show your power against these who would steal me from your kingdom! Send me great strength to resist those who want me to come away with them! Make me strong against their wills!"

My heart was wrung for Bob who had been so thankful for his freedom. Sweat stood out on his forehead. Jack, too, was looking with compassion at the kneeling figure. It appeared that God's Spirit had at least momentarily freed Jack.

Bob suddenly leaped to his feet and faced me squarely. "I'm back! I told you I'd be back! You thought you had my boys all wrapped up, didn't you?"

Jack flashed a pleading look at me. I could hear Betsy praying in the other room. Everything in me was crying out to the Lord for help.

Bob turned to Jack and pointed a commanding finger at him. "You, boy! What are you doing here? You're mine! You're going to burn in hell with the rest of us!"

I concentrated in prayer with all the strength I had. God's authority in my voice drew Bob's eyes to me. "In the name and power of Jesus Christ and his blood shed on Calvary, I command you to leave this boy!" I shouted.

"What's happening?" Bob asked, immediately freed. But before I could sigh in relief Jack was laughing horribly.

"I've come for you both," the voice in Jack insisted.

The demon had either moved from Bob to Jack, or there were two. *"That's* what's happening, Bob," I warned, pointing to Jack. "A second ago it was you. Now it's him."

Bob was like a frightened child. "I thought they were gone. You told me they were gone," he whimpered.

"They *can* be, Bob. You've got to ask Jesus in . . ." But Bob was gone again.

"Anyone for tag?" he kidded. "I'm here!"

"I'm here," the same voice echoed in Jack.

And they laughed together.

I was determined not to give in. I knew that the power was available to send them away, and I shouted, "In the name and power of Jesus Christ, I command you both to go!"

Bob and Jack looked at each other, and then at me. I prayed aloud, "Lord, please, let me talk with them, please!"

Bob looked terribly dejected. Jack looked confused. But they seemed to be themselves.

The air in the room felt cold and I knew I had to talk fast.

"Now look, guys, I don't know how much time we have, so I'm going to give it to you straight. It looks like years of being used by these demons has made it easy for them to come back. Now, I sure don't know very much about this kind of thing, but I *do* know that they run from the name of Jesus. And that means just what it's always meant: that your only hope is to ask him to free you. It's spiritual power against spiritual power, guys, and there's no hope of winning outside of Jesus Christ himself!"

Bob broke the silence that followed. "But I already *did*. And what good did it do?"

Before I could answer, Jack's face changed. "*No* good! That's what! No good. Because there isn't enough power in the universe to stop me!"

Bob was terrified! Jack's twisted expression was sinister. I broke in desperately.

"You see, Bob? That's just what he looks like when he's

in you!" I pushed at him. "Call on Jesus now, Bob, while you can!"

But it was already too late. "Call on him while you can!" mocked the voice, significantly without the name of Jesus in his statement.

"Why don't you give up?" Bob's voice was a sneer.

"Yeah," Jack picked it up. "Why don't you give up?"

But Betsy had called the Gibsons, and all three were praying earnestly together on the phone.

"I'll get you, too, Tim. And Betsy, too. And Jesse! I'll get all of you before I'm finished!" one of them shouted.

"We're children of God!" I shot back. "We were born into his kingdom! We belong to him, and he won't let you hurt any of us! You were beaten at Calvary! Remember?"

"Beat! Me? I'm far from beat! I'm going to win! Just wait and see! I'm going to win!"

"You're a liar, Satan! The Bible says it. You're a liar!"

"I'm *not . . . a* liar!" he shouted arrogantly. "I am the *king of lies!* The king of lies!"

Our encounter grew increasingly bizarre. One moment we were struggling for the souls of the brothers, the next bickering about theology, the next they'd be barking or howling or behaving obscenely. My mind shouted, "Lord, help! Please!"

Finally, Bob lunged at me, and tried to bite my leg. I side-stepped and fell on him in an attempt to restrain him. But he was in an awkward position, and my fall brought our combined weight down hard on his wrist. I heard a snap, and Bob yelled in pain!

"My wrist! My wrist is broken," he shouted. "What are you doing? Get off me! My wrist!"

At that precise moment on the telephone in the next room, Betsy and the Gibsons were asking God for a miracle on my behalf.

Bob remained on the floor, holding his aching wrist. Jack was on a chair, head in his hands, exhausted. Slowly I pulled myself off the floor, feeling utterly drained.

The encounter was over. The Lord had stopped it. The boys were themselves, and we had Bob's throbbing wrist, the overturned furniture, and our disheveled appearances as evidence a storm had passed through.

"Wow," Jack murmured, shaking his head.

"I think my wrist is broken," Bob whined from the floor.

"I gotta get outa here." Jack said, lifting his tired body from the chair.

"I'm going with you," Bob said, and he raised his good hand for assistance. Jack pulled him up, and together they started for the door.

"Hey, fellas," I tried to call, but my voice cracked. "Don't you understand how important it is to get right with the Lord? Now?"

"Later, huh, Tim?" Jack said over his shoulder. "We gotta get it together."

And they departed, walking close together like broken derelicts.

"Now what?" The sound of Betsy's voice startled me.

"I . . . I don't know," I admitted. "But it can't be over. We can't give up on them. And it's sure that Satan isn't going to, either. I just don't know."

8

It's His Battle

The next two days were tranquil, but every time the phone rang at home or in my office my mind asked, "Is this it?" In our time together in the evening, Betsy and I began to put the events of the past few days on paper, comparing memories, feelings, and trying to examine the facts. We had many questions. Why hadn't the casting out of Bob's guardians been successful? Why hadn't Jack remained free from his possessor? Was there something more we should have done?

On the morning of the third day, Betsy answered the phone during breakfast and I saw her tighten up. "Oh, hello, Bob," she said with forced cheer. "How are you?" I moved quietly to the extension phone in our bedroom.

". . . spent a lot of time yesterday afternoon with the Lord," Bob was saying as I lifted the receiver. "I got to thinking about a lot of the things you've said. You know, about Jesus and freedom and all that. It made sense all over, and I asked him to come into my life. I said I was sorry for thinking he couldn't handle things the other day."

"That . . . that's just great, Bob. How do you . . . feel?"

"I feel really great. But there's something else."

"What's that?"

"Well, you know my hurt hand?"

"Your wrist?"

"Yeah. It was all swollen and really hurt right through yesterday. And every time I started trying to think about God 'n' everything, it started hurting all the more. Kept me up most of the night."

"That's too bad."

"No, it isn't. Really. 'Cause I got to thinking that my hurt wrist was the way I was supposed to be *kept from* thinking about Jesus. You know, like the devil used to do? So y' know what I did?"

"What?"

"Just what you think: I prayed about it. I asked Jesus to heal my wrist and let me think about him. And know what?"

"He did it?"

"Right on!"

I heard Betsy laugh in delight. "You mean your wrist is completely normal? No swelling? Nothing?"

"Yeah."

"Bob, you don't know how terrific this makes me feel. I know Tim will be thrilled, too. Praise the Lord!"

I couldn't admit I was eavesdropping, so I just nodded and smiled.

Betsy seemed to pause for a moment. "Uh, how's your brother? How's Jack?"

"I think he's in pretty good shape, too. We talked about it some. He feels a little bit like I do. If there's a way to get out from under all our trouble, why not try it?"

I could hear the joy in Betsy's voice. "Are you boys planning on stopping over later?"

"If it's okay. I mean, we kinda messed up your place last time we were there."

"It's back together. And you're welcome."

"We'll see you later. Thanks."

Betsy promised to call the minute they arrived. We thought it would be best if I'd leave the office and come home. But when she didn't call by ten that morning, I called her. In fact, I spent a lot of time that day on the phone with her, checking to be sure everything was all right. The boys didn't show up.

We were just settling down after supper when Bob and Jack arrived, relaxed and grinning.

"She just doesn't know what to do with us," Jack was talking about his mother. "She said she was gonna call the state mental health office about us just a couple of days ago, but now she says we're such *angels* she figures they'd laugh at her."

We all laughed. I was surprised at Jack's expansiveness.

"I think I might have actually made a friend today," Bob smiled. "A guy where I'm working. He . . ."

"I didn't know you had a job," I interrupted.

"Oh, yeah," Bob responded proudly. "Since yesterday. It isn't much now, but if I stick with it I can really move up."

Angels? A steady job? It was almost too good to be true. Maybe God was trying to say that it really was *his* battle; that it didn't depend on us for the victory.

"That's when I got my wrist healed," Bob went on. "I just got the job, and I was going to have to call in sick 'cause I couldn't work with it that way. And then I thought, 'Why don't I just give the Lord a try here?' And I did. And he did!"

We all laughed again. It was hard to believe that these were the same two boys. Betsy and I felt like pinching each other to make sure we were awake.

"Hey, what's this?" The question was casual, and came from Jack. He had Betsy's notebook in his hand. It had been open on the desk, and he had spotted his name on the page.

"Oh, Tim and I were just trying to write down the events of the last few days," Betsy said lightly. "Maybe you should read it and see if you think it matches what happened."

It was a casual invitation, and Jack began to read. Bob moved to look over Jack's shoulder. Jack read aloud. It was an unusual experience, to say the least! Here they were, telling their own story!

Jack began with enthusiasm, enjoying the descriptions of his brother and himself. But as he read, his tone changed. He began skipping words. Not just random words, but specific words. Some of the sentences didn't make any sense at all. Bob leaned over for a closer look, puzzled by the nonsense sentences.

"Hey, Jack," Bob said with a smile. "What are you doing? You're leaving out words. You skipped over 'Jesus' right there."

"Oh. Did I? Light's bad."

The light wasn't bad, and Bob told him so with a forced laugh.

"I'm not feeling so good," Jack said in a strangled voice. The beads of perspiration forming on his forehead and the paleness in his face backed up his statement. It was a familiar pattern, and Betsy and I began to feel a tremendous dread of what was coming. Bob instinctively moved away, and sat down apprehensively.

Jack continued to read. Now he wasn't simply leaving out the words "Lord," "Savior," and "Jesus Christ." He was substituting his own name in their places!

"You've really overplayed your hand this time," I said evenly.

"What are you talking about?" he replied, a look of innocence on his face.

"Jack's going to read that manuscript." I continued, speaking to the spirit inside Jack. "He's going to know what you've been putting him through. And he's going to be free of you by the mighty power of Jesus Christ."

"Do you still think you're a match for me?" Jack suddenly shouted. Jumping to his feet he threw the notebook across the room. We were face-to-face again.

But this encounter was different. I felt the strength of

the Spirit of God in me. It's hard to put the feeling into words, but I knew that Jesus was there.

"No," I said quietly, "one thing these last few days have showed me is that Betsy and I are no match for you."

A smile crept across Jack's face. But before his voice could be used for further words, I continued, "But I've learned another thing just as clearly: *You* are no match for my Lord, Jesus Christ. You don't scare me any more, demon. Greater is he that is in me than you could ever be."

As I said this, a strange look came across Jack's face. His possessor knew I was not bluffing. He knew that the power of God confronted him. For the first time he looked frightened. The expression had the same quality as all the others; it was as though Jack's face was only being used. But it was expressing fear. And my faith, and Betsy's faith, and the mustard seed of faith inside Bob mushroomed. "And now," I said, still quiet in the Lord, "in the name and power of Jesus Christ, I command you to leave this boy . . . *both* these boys . . . *forever.*" There was a moment of frozen silence.

And he was gone. Jack rubbed his face like a man coming indoors out of the icy cold. He seemed to be rubbing it just to get it moving again. He rubbed, and then smiled. He was free.

A few weeks went by with no more manifestations of evil. The boys seemed to be stabilizing. They had periods of doubt, and confusion, and they had to handle a difficult attitude at home, but they were free from possession. We spent many hours with them, reading the Bible, studying about the Source of real strength against evil, and the boys as well as Betsy and I were responding. Jack carried a New Testament in his back pocket, and from its condition I gathered he spent a great deal of time reading it.

Bob's job was working out, but with more difficulty than he'd expected. He had great trouble coping with authority figures, and there were many ahead of him on the promotional ladder. But to his credit, he stuck with it.

Then one afternoon Bob arrived at the house during work

hours. Betsy was surprised to see him, but invited him in. He had cut his knee and said he couldn't go back to work until it was healed. He was depressed and in some pain, and seemed to need a shoulder to cry on.

They talked for a while over coffee, and Betsy suggested he have his doctor order something for the pain. He left the house in about the same emotional state as he had arrived.

Later that evening Jack came for the Bible study we had arranged earlier. "Bob couldn't make it. His knee was killing him."

"Didn't he get anything for the pain?" Betsy asked sympathetically.

"Yeah. The doctor gave him some capsules. He took two or three of 'em but they didn't seem to do anything. He's feeling pretty low."

"Two or three? What did he say?"

"I don't know. Something about that he'd had it. He said nothing was gonna work out right anyway, so he might as well split."

"What does he mean?" I was beginning to get a little worried about more than Bob's pain.

"I don't know." Jack's reply was glib. "He gets like that once in a while. He'll feel better later."

"But with all that pain-killer in his system . . ." Betsy never finished her sentence. The phone rang. It was Bob. He spoke in chopped phrases insisting he would only talk to Jack.

Jack listened after his initial, "Hi," and then put the phone down. "Can I talk to him somewhere else?"

"Sure," I answered, trying not to see the worry in Betsy's eyes. "There's a phone in the bedroom."

Jack left the room. I walked to the phone, intending to hang it up as soon as I heard their voices. Of course, I was curious as to what the call might be about, but I intended to hang up. As I lifted the receiver to replace it, I heard Bob saying, "Remember me the way we are on that picture of us at Grandma's. You can make it, Jack. I know you can. Don't get all messed up like me."

It sounded like a final kind of farewell. Impulsively I lifted the receiver the rest of the way and intruded. "Where are you, Bob?" My voice surprised me. It was too loud and tense.

"I don't want to talk to you. I've had it!" There was a click at the other end. Betsy, Jack, and I seemed immediately to know what to do. In a matter of minutes, we were in the car, cruising through areas of town we knew Bob liked.

"I still don't think he's going to do anything stupid," Jack was saying.

But I had other feelings. My mind kept hearing threats like, "If I can't have him, I'll kill him! You haven't won yet! I'm still going to win!"

"Lord, lead us to him. Help us find him." Betsy's fervent prayer spoke for us all.

"Look!" Jack suddenly shouted, pointing to a hamburger stand ahead on the right. "There's his bike."

Parked at the restaurant was a familiar-looking 350, but it was impossible to tell whether Bob was inside the building. I eased the car into the parking lot, and we got out, our eyes racing over the scene in an effort to glimpse Bob. Dead end. A closer look at the bike was all Jack needed to confirm that it wasn't his brother's. We raced back into the car, and were agonizing for a break in traffic when, "There he is!" Betsy shouted.

We all gasped. It was Bob, all right, full throttle, weaving through the heavy traffic, looking as though he was *trying* to cause an accident! I pulled out after him, almost causing an accident myself, and did the best I could to keep him in view. If he had been driving straight, he would have lost us easily, but his weaving kept the distance between us at a constant rate.

"He's just trying to get up the nerve," Jack said with quiet, knowing sympathy.

Then, suddenly, Bob sped off onto a dirt side road. The road led to a large land-fill area which was presently being used as a garbage dump.

We were off the road and right behind him. At the speed

we were going, the headlights gave us little warning about the chuck-holes we bounced through. We were thrown around, but none of us seemed to notice. Our attention was on the single red taillight ahead.

Then it was gone! "He must have turned off somewhere," Jack shouted over the thumping of our bouncing car.

"I don't know where he could," I shouted back. "I've been up here before. There just isn't anywhere to . . ." And then I saw what he had done.

In the rear-view mirror, I saw Bob pull back out onto the road, and head back toward the highway. He had simply pulled his little 350 off, hidden behind a bush, and waited for us to pass. There was nowhere on the road large enough to do that with a car.

I raced to the dumping area and spun the car around. We then bumped and roared back toward the highway. If Bob was planning to kill himself, he'd had plenty of time to get far enough away to do it.

As the highway came into view, we could see that traffic had increased to a bumper-to-bumper density. It was maintaining a decent speed, but trying to break into that line of cars was going to be almost impossible.

"Oh, man," Jack moaned. "We lost him."

I was afraid that might be prophetic.

"No, we haven't," Betsy suddenly chirped. "Look!"

And there, just outside the reach of our headlights, watching the traffic go by, was Bob. He was still sitting on his bike, but the motor and lights were off. He was just sitting and staring.

"You okay?" I asked, running toward him.

"I don't know what got into me," he said three or four times. "I just don't know. I was really gonna do it. I wasn't putting you on. I really was gonna do it. And then when I saw it was you chasing me, instead of cops like I thought, I just said, 'What am I doing here?' "

We talked for a while and then all drove back to our house for coffee and prayers of thanksgiving for the Lord's leading and rescue.

Bob and Jack still have real problems. The devil is not content over losing two souls. But since the last times I've described here, neither of the boys has been actually oppressed by an evil spirit.

Today Bob has trouble believing that all of it really happened to him. He was never aware of his possessing spirits when they were expressing themselves. Jack, on the other hand, knew he was controlled by an evil presence, and is more and more joyful to be free in Christ.

The brothers now live together in a small apartment, and both show signs of increasing stability. They are still up and down emotionally. And they still vacillate between belief and doubt in a practical Christian way. But the old hate, which was once so much a part of their lives, is gone. And it looks as though Jesus Christ is in the process of healing their hearts and minds.

As for Betsy and me, we too are stabilizing. We were exposed to so much, taught so much in such a short time, that the experience is still settling.

We met Bob and Jack when we were a Christian couple with a rather complacent, logical world-view. We had experienced salvation, of course, but our Christian life was a down-to-earth, day-by-day, ordinary kind of living. There was little room for what we couldn't understand. And we were unprepared to be thrown face-first into conflict with the raw powers of evil.

We slowly discovered how little we really knew of the Scriptures. Sure, they are described in the book of Ephesians as the "sword" in the battle against evil, but when Betsy and I first went to battle we were practically unarmed!

We learned a few things about faith, too. I think we were in the same place as many Christians who have a kind of faith *in their own faith*. We discovered that it is faith in *Jesus Christ* that has value. We had to let go of ourselves.

And, most of all, we were awakened to a powerful God. A loving God who, it seems now, we little knew then. We found him to be all power, all love, all concern. He is able, and even more exciting, he loves. And because of his love, his power is working in our behalf. It isn't hard to have a childlike faith in a God like that.

Betsy and I have asked ourselves many times why we faced so many setbacks in our work with the brothers. As we looked in God's Word, we were startled by the story in Matthew 17. A father brings a demon-possessed boy to Jesus with the report that the disciples had tried but failed to free him. After casting the demon out, Jesus tells the disciples that the reason they couldn't do it was their *lack of faith*. This kind of a demon, Jesus adds, won't go out without prayer and fasting.

Betsy and I weren't prepared in the beginning for the kind of spiritual war we found ourselves in. Gradually, we came to see the seriousness of the struggle and the spiritual resources needed. We are sure that God wants every Christian to be prepared for any kind of battle he must fight with the evil one, but that preparation must include a vigorous, day-by-day, total commitment.

We learned the hard way about the spiritual forces opposing Christians. Perhaps the Lord chose us because we were so typical of many Christians who find it hard to take the spiritual, unseen world as a literal reality. Maybe the telling of our story is part of his plan to alert you.

There are two portions of Scripture that have become part of us through this experience. I don't feel there is any better way to close the story than with them.

Be careful — watch out for attacks from Satan, your great enemy. He prowls around like a hungry, roaring lion, looking for some victim to tear apart. Stand firm when he attacks. Trust the Lord . . . (*1 Peter 5:8, 9*).

Last of all I want to remind you that your strength must come from the Lord's mighty power within you. Put on all of God's armor so that you will be able to stand safe against all strategies and tricks of Satan. For we are not fighting against people made of flesh and blood, but against persons without bodies — the evil rulers of the unseen world, those mighty satanic beings and great evil princes of darkness who rule this world; and against huge numbers of wicked spirits in the spirit world.

So use every piece of God's armor to resist the enemy whenever he attacks, and when it is all over, you will still be standing up.

But to do this, you will need the strong belt of truth, and the breastplate of God's approval. Wear shoes that are able to speed you on as you preach the Good News of peace with God. In every battle you will need faith as your shield to stop the fiery arrows aimed at you by Satan. And you will need the helmet of salvation and the sword of the Spirit — which is the Word of God.

Pray all the time. Ask God for anything in line with the Holy Spirit's wishes. Plead with him, reminding him of your needs, and keep praying for all Christians everywhere (*Ephesians 6:10-18*).

Praise the Lord!